How much money is being unapproachable costing you?

FACT #1

The only judgment
people can (honestly)
make about you is how
interacting with *you*
makes *them* FEEL.

FACT #2

If you're not *perceived* and *remembered* as being approachable by the people you serve – I guarantee you (and your organization) will suffer.

LESSON LEARNED:

Approachability becomes profitability.

So, before learning how to become an approachable leader, I invite you to consider these impending dangers of UN-approachability as a cautionary primer:

When you're unapproachable, people will plan ways to avoid you. Which,
ironically, takes more time and energy than actually talking to you. But that's how we're wired: Anthropologically, the more conflict that's possible, the more we avoid that encounter. Even if it requires more work. *How many people went out of their way to avoid you yesterday?*

When you're unapproachable, people will shrink from opportunities to be open. If you're the kind of person who takes offense to everything, for example,
here's what happens. People will start tiptoeing around you, trying their hardest not to get caught in your vortex of hypersensitivity. Then, they'll purposely leave out key points just to avoid pushing your hot buttons. And all that does is leave you in the dark on where they stand. *How many relationship problems are you currently unaware of because your emotional reactivity silences people?*

When you're unapproachable, people will be surprised by your arguments and concerns. Because you weren't proactive enough to share your
expectations clearly and early. Or because you didn't speak with Meaningful Concrete Immediacy. Or because you shaded the truth. As someone who's screwed this one up royally in his own life, take it from me: When people become accustomed to living in the dark, it surprises the hell out of them when the lights suddenly flicker on. *Are your expectations camouflaged?*

When you're unapproachable, people will stop volunteering information.
Because they won't feel that being around you is a safe container in which they can share. Which means they'll either bury their problems deep down inside their bodies (which causes physical stress), or take their problems to someone else (who probably has no idea what the hell they're talking about). *How are you creating a Question Friendly Environment?*

When you're unapproachable, people will become apprehensive due to your unpredictability. If people never know what's on your mind, the silent dialogue
will become, "For all I know, he could be a ticking time bomb this morning! Better not say anything deep or lengthy." Again, this leads to low-involvement conversations with minimal self-disclosure. And because nobody knows what you're thinking, they (might) end up doing the exact opposite of what you wanted. And it will be YOUR fault because, contrary to your hopes and dreams, they were unable to read your mind. *What are you doing that prevents people from learning from you?*

When you're unapproachable, people will be on guard around you.
Because they feel tense. Self-conscious. Afraid to offend you. Walking on eggshells. Hesitant to set off your emotions. And the mental energy they expend on those fear-based thoughts (1) robs them of their ability to be true, (2) prevents them from offering full information, and (3) scares them away from sharing what's most important. *What questions are your employees afraid to ask you?*

When you're unapproachable, people will be at a loss of words around you. Because you make them nervous. Because you don't give them permission. Because you aren't making communication a relaxing experience. *How easy is it for people to open up around you?*

When you're unapproachable, people will feel like a non-person around you. Especially if unnecessary titles prevent them from getting to know you authentically. Also, if unspoken hierarchies exist, take caution. This hampers the freedom of expression and creates psychological distance between people. No matter how "open" (you say) your door really is. *Are you treating people like people or statistics?*

When you're unapproachable, people will feel tense or nervous around you. Which causes them stress. Which corrodes their health. Which impairs their positive attitude. Which lowers their overall performance. Which loses the organization money. *Are exhausting to be around?*

When you're unapproachable, people will hold (mostly) shallow interactions. And your communication topics will always remain superficial. Nobody will ever get to the heart of any important issues because they're holding back, unsure about how you might react. As a result, very little ever gets accomplished. *Do you really think asking about traffic or the weather is an effective conversation starter?*

When you're unapproachable, people will perceive interactions with as being longer. And, therefore, uncomfortable. As such, most interactions will end prematurely because people will want to get the hell out of there as soon as possible. Ultimately, this reputation will contaminate the space that surrounds you. *How could you make the time spent with you seem shorter?*

When you're unapproachable, people walk away with self-esteem damage. Because when you don't respond objectively, openly and curiously to their ideas, people feel less intelligent after talking to you. Eventually, they find themselves not wanting to talk to you. And sadly, people will almost feel at peace or relieved if they haven't talked to you in a while. All because you never took the time to consider "how you leave people." *What invisible walls have your close-minded attitude built?*

When you're unapproachable, people walk away feeling deflated. And they'll feel that things are hopeless after being around you. This corrodes motivation and hampers commitment. Which lowers their performance. Which heightens animosity. Which makes loyalty vanish. Yikes. *How often do you inspire people to inspire themselves?*

When you're unapproachable, people walk away emotionally numb. Because they were never given permission to relax, be their true selves and exert their distinctiveness. They were forced into compliance. They were haphazardly labeled ENFJ and then stored in a nice little, predictable box. This is what happens if people feel constantly judged by you. Or if you take issue or ague with everything they say. They perceive your value system to be SO opposed that your ego won't allow you to listen to them. Eventually, they won't bother approaching you at all. And that's when you, as a leader, miss out on their valuable ideas, opportunities and feedback. *How often do you overlook people who might offer meaningful ideas?*

When you're unapproachable, people walk away having missed opportunities for growth.
Without mental flexibility and openness, here's what happens: People stop learning, which means people stop growing, which means people start dying. Yikes. Not good for business. *How do you add value to people?*

When you're unapproachable, people will walk away feeling devalued.
Especially if you didn't monopolize the listening and make them feel essential. And eventually, they might start asking themselves, "Why do I even bother talking to her anyway?" *How do people experience themselves in relation to you?*

When you're unapproachable, people walk aware worse.
Kind of the opposite of the old hiking rule, "Leave the camp sight better than the way you found it." In this case, people are in a bad mood after being around you. Which kinds of makes them NOT want to be around you very often. And, when they ARE around you, it results in curt communication underscored by a lack of mindfulness because all they're thinking about his how badly they want the conversation to be over. *Are people diminished, unaffected, or enlarged after their encounter with you?*

Sorry. Didn't mean to scare you. I just thought you might like to know the cost of being unapproachable. So, here's the deal: I'm willing to change if you are. Cool?

The Approachable Leader

Scott Ginsberg
Copyright © 2010 HELLO, my name is Scott!

Printed in the United States of America.

Cover design by
Sue Sylvia of Staircase Press Design

Text layout by
Jeff Braun of TriFecta Creative
www.trifectacreative.com

Edited by
Jessica "That Bagel Girl" Adams

ISBN: 978-0-9726497-9-7

"Eat this book one bite at a time - it's delicious!"
— Arthur Scharff, Founder, AAIM Presidents' & Leadership Council

INCLUDES
The
CONSISTENCY
Audit™

HELLO, my name is Scott's...

THE
APPROACHABLE
LEADER

SQUAW

QUACK

MEEP

49 Daily Practices for Inspiring, Influencing
and Infecting Your Followers

... From the guy who made a career
out of wearing a nametag

Scott Ginsberg

Table of Contents

one   What does your Open Door Policy (actually) prove? 12

two   What if you implemented an Open Mind Policy? 15

three   When you walk into a room how does it change? 18

four   Who wants to sit in your radius? 21

five   How do people experience you? 25

six   Is there a gap between your onstage
performance and backstage reality? 32

seven   How are you making communication a relaxing experience? 35

eight   Are you the most inspirational person you know? 39

nine   How are you leaving a permanent imprint on people? 46

ten   How are people changed after having a conversation with you? 48

eleven   Are you leading from the heart or the handbook? 51

twelve   Are you willing to bean imperfectionist? 54

thirteen   How are you leveraging your vulnerability to earn people's trust? 60

fourteen   How will you fully integrate your humanity into your position? 69

fifteen   How could you inspire and influence through inadequacy? 73

sixteen   What fuels the engine of your credibility? 79

seventeen   How are you branding your honesty? 82

eighteen   How do you honor the spirit in those you serve? 87

nineteen   How listenable are you? 93

twenty   What's preventing your ideas from getting through? 102

twenty-one   How will you raise the receptivity of those you serve? 105

twenty-two   How does your playfulness product profit? 110

twenty-three   How many relationships are you missing out
on because you don't know people's names? 114

twenty-four   How beautifully do you treat people? 118

twenty-five   How are you making people feel essential? 120

twenty-six   Are you listening or anticipating? 124

Table of Contents

twenty-seven How do you assist others in giving birth to their own understanding? 127

twenty-eight How are you helping people lead themselves? 130

twenty-nine Are you willing to go on a listening expedition? 132

thirty What are the two simple words that INSTANTLY make you a great listener? 135

thirty-one How are you building a reputation as an askable person? 142

thirty-two Are people coming to you for help? 148

thirty-three What's the most dangerous question any leader could ask? 153

thirty-four How do you respond when people fall out of posture? 155

thirty-five How challenging are you willing to be? 159

thirty-six How are you painting a compelling vision of the future? 161

thirty-seven Are you leading or coaching? 164

thirty-eight What is affecting your ability to be taken seriously? 170

thirty-nine Do people have to be careful what they say around you? 174

forty Do your employees want to murder you? 179

forty-one Where do you suck? 184

forty-two How much employee loyalty are you sacrificing by being unapproachable? 187

forty-three What will be your legacy of openness? 191

forty-four Have you ever audited your consistency? 196

forty-five If you were the most consistent person you knew, how would your organization be different? 201

forty-six How do you make decisions? 205

forty-seven What if you practiced everything? 208

forty-eight When you walk out of a room, how does it change? 217

forty-nine How do you leave people? 221

HELLO
MY NAME IS CHAPTER,

one

What does your Open Door Policy (actually) prove?

"I don't understand why people think I'm unapproachable. I HAVE an open door policy…!

OK, well, that may be true. Your door may be open.

But the REAL question people want to know the answer to is…

Is your MIND open? Is your HEART open? And are your EARS open?

Because if they're not, I don't care if you surgically remove the door from your wall. That still doesn't reduce the psychological distance between you and the people around you.

So, whether you're interacting with employees, clients, guests, attendees, colleagues, members, congregants, friends and students – even your own kids – the same universal principle of approachability applies.

See, it takes much more than an "open door policy" or "regular office hours" or "body language that signals your willingness to take an interest in the other person and listen with the intent to understand, not be understood."

Look, no offense, but that simplistic Communication 101 crap isn't going cut it anymore.

HERE'S THE REALITY: If you want to give people permission to...

Come up TO...
Feel relaxed AROUND...
Open up WITH...
Comfortably walk away FROM, and
Confidently return TO you...

...You need to open more than just the door.

Approachability derives from the Latin word *apropiare*, or "to come nearer to."

Which means being approachable is a combination of three factors:

FIRST: The openness and attractiveness of your <u>personal being</u> as a function of your attitudes, values and core selfhood.

SECOND: The openness and attractiveness of your <u>physical space</u> as a function of your language, behaviors and environment.

THIRD: The openness and attractiveness of your <u>public persona</u> as a function of your reputation, personal brand and visibility.

Your challenge is to narrow the gap. To melt away the layers that clog, contaminate or close off the communication channels between you and ... *whoever.*

Here's a common example.

Imagine an employee walks into your office. She offers a quick hello, sits down and then asks if she can discuss a problem she's having with one of her coworkers.

Now, as a manager, there are certain questions you'd want to ask. Probably certain emotional reactions you'd want to avoid. And definitely certain listening behaviors you'd want to exhibit.

Still, under the surface of those *mechanical* practices, something deeper and stronger would be at work too.

REMEMBER: Approachability originates from your core. *Your truth. Your personhood. Your most honest and vulnerable self.*

And it is only when you're willing to exert that core that you can TRULY be hospitable to the soul of the person sitting across from you.

This, of course, is hard to do. I speak from my experience as an author, speaker and coach – not to mention the only person in the world who's worn a nametag 24-7 for the past ten years.

In fact, I've identified five reasons WHY being approachable is hard:

1. **Approachability is hard because it requires AWARENESS.**
   Recognizing the other person's values without violating them. Responding and attending to their immediate experience without judgment, evaluation or immediate appraisal.

2. **Approachability is hard because it requires HONESTY.**
   Telling the truth, honoring your truth and respecting other people's truths. And breaking down the barriers to your authenticity.

3. **Approachability is hard because it requires OPENNESS.**
   Greeting new ideas with a welcoming, vulnerable heart. Listening without defending, fixing, interrupting, rehearsing or anticipating.

4. **Approachability is hard because it requires LETTING GO.**
   Of your ego. Of your need to be right. Of your desire to annoyingly decorate the conversation with your clever little jokes.

5. **Approachability is hard because it requires CONSISTENCY.**
   Staying congruent and true to your boundaries and values. Remembering that consistency is far better than rare moments of greatness.

Just because you're accessible doesn't mean you're approachable.

Just because the door is open doesn't mean people are going to walk in.

If you want to give people permission to come up to, feel relaxed around, open up with, comfortably walk away from, and confidently return to you, you need to open more than just the door.

HELLO
MY NAME IS CHAPTER,

two

What if you implemented an Open Mind Policy?

Doors are for amateurs.

Approachable leaders need open MINDS.

Here are four suggestions for implementing and Open Mind Policy:

1. **Create an environment of openness.** *As you recall, people need to feel they've been given PERMISSION to (1) come up to, (2) feel relaxed around, (3) open up with, (4) comfortably walk away from, and (5) confidently return to you.*

   PRACTICE: Don't be too busy to explain anything. If that's the perception people maintain of you, you've communicated two dangerous messages: (1) Your time is more valuable than theirs, and (2) Their question is not important.

   Stop whatever you're doing and give yourself fully to the other person. Or, if they people catch you off guard, book "blank time" in your schedule so people know for certain when they can get you.

   Another suggestion is to post a "Lunch with Mark" sign-up sheet outside your office or on your door. Let people choose the day that best fits their schedule. That way they can come shoot the breeze with you on an informal, unstructured, non-threatening, one-on-one basis. The probability of opening up will immediately increase.

   LET ME ASK YA THIS: How do you initiate movement toward people?

2. **Be someone who can be trusted with sensitive information.** *Becoming someone that anybody can tell anything will reduce the likelihood of everyone kicking you to the curb.*

    PRACTICE: Exercise confidentiality when dealing with sensitive issues. Create a Question Friendly Environment (QFE.) A safe space. A non-threatening atmosphere where people (1) feel comfortable, and (2) feel like they have permission to ask anything that's on their minds.

    Consider trashing your "Suggestion Box" and replace it with a "Question Box." Honesty will flourish. Feedback will flow like wine. Especially if people don't have to sign their names, as anonymity increases dissociation and, therefore, increases honesty.

    LET ME ASK YA THIS: Do people feel safe around you?

3. **Engage in more "What if?" discussions.** *Approachable leaders are giant question marks.*

    PRACTICE: There are only two possible responses to a "What if?" discussion: Either you pause and openly consider the question with an attitude of curiosity and enthusiasm – or you reflexively launch into a defensive routine of "Yeah, but…" backpedaling in order to preserve your precious ego.

    And the challenge is, ONE of those response patterns draws people TO you, while the other repels people FROM you. I wonder which one YOU practice. Perhaps a sticky note with a giant X through the words, "Yeah, but…" would reinforce this behavior.

    LET ME ASK YA THIS: What words govern your questions?

4. **Eagerly pursue new knowledge, skills, and methods.** *Approachability is a function of teachability.*

    PRACTICE: In the book *Counterfeit Leadership,* Ken Shelton explains, "Continuous learning is the best protection against pride. A person who is vigorously learning can't be egotistical about what he or she knows, because each increase in understanding reveals a larger area of ignorance."

The secret to being teachable is daring to be dumm. Demonstrating a willingness to put your ego on the shelf and approach everyone and everything as your teacher, mentor and resource. Without such mental flexibility and openness, here's what happens: You stop learning, which means you stop growing, which means you start dying. *Yikes.* Not good for business. We'll talk more about this later.

LET ME ASK YA THIS: How many books did you read last month?

REMEMBER: Doors are meaningless. Try opening your mind first.

HELLO
MY NAME IS CHAPTER,

three

When you walk into a room how does it change?

TWO WORDS: Michael Scott.

If you watch NBC's *The Office,* you know what I mean.

Poor Michael. As the branch manager of Dunder Mifflin, every time he walks into the room, something bad happens.

People stare.
People stop talking.
People walk the other way.

Even in one particular episode, one of his employee's stress monitor started beeping faster and faster as Michael approached him.

Yikes.

What about you? When you walk into a room, how does it change?

For the most part, this reaction isn't under your direct control.

Whatever change occurs to the room is a tangible representation of how your character, actions, words, reputation and personality have both preceded and affected the people around you.

The following list explores several possibilities of how a room might change when you walk in the door. As you explore these examples, ask yourself which of them best applies to you, or which ones you'd LIKE to apply to you:

1. **Does your entrance shift the dialogue UP?** If so, that could mean a few things: (1) people love to greet you, (2) people were just talking about you – probably positively – and now they've escalated the conversation because they're excited to involve you, or (3) people were just talking about a particular topic they would LOVE to get your thoughts or opinion on.

   RESULT: Everyone is engaged, creating excitement in the air.

2. **Does your entrance shift the dialogue DOWN?** If so, that could mean a few things: (1) people were just talking about you – probably negatively – but now they've stopped the conversation for fear of getting busted, (2) people were just talking about a particular topic they either don't want – or are afraid to ask – your opinion on.

   RESULT: Everyone is walking on eggshells; creating anxiety in the air.

3. **Do people stare?** If so, that could mean a few things: (1) something about your attractiveness – either physical or psychological – catches their eye, (2) something about your memorable presence and unique personal style immediately captivates their attention, (3) they were just talking about you - either positively or negatively – and now they can't help but burn a hole in the back of your shirt.

   RESULT: You become The Observed, not The Observer.

4. **Are they curious or wondering about you?** In this case, they're not really staring, yet they *are* noticing you. If so, that could mean a few things: (1) you look like an interesting person, maybe because you're smiling, laughing, or just appear fascinating and intriguing; (2) you're wearing something unexpected that breaks their normal pattern of observation.

   RESULT: You create a Point of Dissonance that increases the likelihood of an encounter.

5. **Do they start buzzing about you?** In this instance, people have heard about you. They've seen your name before. They might even recognize your face from a website, publication or video interview. Either way, they *are* talking about you. Could be good or bad. So, just remember the words of Oscar Wilde: "The only thing worse than being talked about is NOT being talked about."

   RESULT: Word of Mouth has sparked.

6. **Do they come up to you?** Some people move shyly in your direction. Others smile and walk towards you. Sometimes a mob of raving fans will run full speed with open arms, hoping to be the first to hug you! Either way, you're approachable. People flock to you. They want to sit in your radius.

   RESULT: You're the kind of person who always has one or two people engaged in your presence.

7. **Do they walk away from you?** *"Oh no, look who's here. I better go into the other room…" "Gotta run. Don't want to be seen by HER…" "Excuse me, but I just can't stand that guy. I need to go outside for a few minutes…"* Wow. Sounds like you laid some low-quality track.

   RESULT: People who DON'T know you begin to question your credibility and character as they observe this "room reaction."

NOTE: These are only a sampling of examples of how a room might change when you walk in. The outcomes will be different for everybody.

The challenge is that this moment of truth when you walk into a room has little to do with the room itself.

REMEMBER: Whatever change occurs to a room as you walk in is a tangible representation of how your character, actions, words, reputation and personality have both preceded and affected the people around you.

So, if you're not satisfied with the reactions you've been getting, don't criticize the room.

Instead, look in the mirror.

HELLO
MY NAME IS CHAPTER,

four

Who wants to sit in your radius?

As a professional speaker, I love watching other speakers do their thing.

Especially the really, really good ones.

EXAMPLE: A few months ago I delivered the keynote address at a recruiting conference. After four standing ovations and three encores (OK, not really) I had some time to kill before my flight back to St. Louis. Now, this doesn't happen to me that often, so I was pretty stoked. I ended up attending a breakout session hosted by my friend Jeff Skrentney.

He's one of the really, really good ones. So, I went to his session not because I wanted to learn or to take notes or get my next million-dollar idea; but rather because Jeff – this cool, successful, wealthy, happy, balanced, healthy, vastly experienced, brilliant man – is someone you just **want to be in the radius of.**

Can you tell I have a bit of a man-crush on him?

Anyway.

Certain people, special people, don't really have to say or do that much. They just have to BE. And in that simple state of being, that existence, they influence you. They change you. They inspire you and teach you.

What about you? Who wants to sit in YOUR radius?

Here's a list of practices, behaviors and actions you can start implementing TODAY to increase the number of people who want to sit in your radius. And while you're reading this list, I'd also like you to be thinking about: (1) whose radius YOU want to sit in, (2) why you want to sit there, and (3) how you can emulate those traits in your own daily life.

1. **Affirm people earlier.** In conversations. In sales calls. In meetings. In relationships. Ensure that people feel validated. *How are you laying a foundation of affirmation?*

2. **Allow people's feelings.** Never under any circumstances say, "You don't really feel that way." People are entitled to feel however they want. You job is to dance in the moment. To respond to their present experience. *When was the last time someone cried in front of you?*

3. **Awaken people's curiosity.** You do this by being curious yourself. By asking killer questions. By finding everything absurdly interesting. Ultimately, when you're passionate about questioning and discovering and exploring, it's contagious. *How many times a day do you say, "Huh … Now THAT'S interesting…"?*

4. **Bring people joy.** If you concentrate on doing this at least three times a day, your life won't just BE swell; it will swell with happiness and purpose. And so will the lives of the people you touch. Try playing the "Let's See How Many People I Can Make Smile Today" game. *How many people did you look in the eye and say thank you to yesterday?*

5. **Capture people's imagination.** Don't give advice; tell stories. Don't puke your boring company history; travel back in time with customers. Don't give lectures; paint pictures. Einstein was right: Imagination is more important than knowledge. *Are you boring people? Bueller? Bueller? Bueller?*

6. **Change people's metaphors.** When you change their metaphors, you change their language. When you change their language, you change their thinking. When you change their thinking, you rock their world. *Whose thinking are you reframing?*

7. **Cheer people on.** The more cheerleaders people have, the easier it is for them to win. For example: Ever seen The Packers play a home game at Lambeau Field in December? IN-sane. Even if the opposing team wins, you KNOW their players were scared shitless the whole time. *Are you that supportive of YOUR people?*

8. **Exhaust people's limits.** Try pushing them a little harder. And a little harder. And a little harder. Don't kill 'em, but challenge people to create new edges for themselves. As my yoga instructor says, "Stretch their bodies and minds and souls to a point where they're not in pain; but where pain is definitely possible." *Whom are YOU stretching?*

9. **Get people involved.** Which is pretty easy to do, once you know what they're passionate about. All you have to do is embed their passion into the pavement that leads the way. Then they'll arrive quicker, healthier, happier and with more ownership because THEY created the path. *Whose passion are you excavating?*

10. **Give people permission.** To share. To open up. To be themselves. To ask questions. To fail. To be wrong. To be ignorant (not stupid, but ignorant.) To make mistakes. To kick ass. To succeed. To win. *What are you giving people permission to do?*

11. **Hear people out.** Another cool game to play is the "Let's See How Long I Can Go Without Speaking" game. It's fun, challenging, healthy and usually results in the other person making creative breakthroughs. *How quickly do you interrupt people?*

12. **Ignore people's titles.** President? CFO? Receptionist? Janitor? Who the hell cares? As a 24-7 nametag wearer for 10+ years, I believe the only label people should EVER be called by is their name. Because they're a human being. Period. Titles alienate people. Titles are overrated. Next time someone asks you something like, "So then, are you a Christian?" reply with, "Nope, I'm a human!" *What unnecessary title is preventing people from getting to know the REAL you?*

13. **Keep people moving.** No movement, no progress. No progress, no money. Period. You've got to get crackin.' Even if it's not much. Infinitesimal as the movement may seem, something is better than nothing. Saddle up, partner! *What happened the last you're your team stopped moving?*

14. **Lead people's thinking.** Be the spark; then shut up and get out of the way. Ask a few key questions; then trust people to tap their inner resources. More than likely, they'll drum up their own solutions that are more accurate, more richly supported, more precise and more THEIRS than whatever you could have come up with for them. *Are you an idea midwife?*

15. **Make people better.** No, wait. I'm wrong. What I meant to say was, "The only person you can make better is yourself." However, in so doing, perhaps

your growth and escalating awesomeness will inspire others. Perhaps your minor improvements will remind them that they can do the same. *Whose personal development are you inspiring?*

16. **Number people's feelings.** Ask them, "On a scale from 1-10, how would you rate your (X)." Sure, it sounds a bit clinical. But it's the best way to gauge their status, get a clear reading, then figure out where to go from there. *How are you objectifying people intangibles?*

17. **Release people's genius.** Constantly create situations that make it easy for people to shine. Steer the conversation into the direction of their passion and expertise, step back and watch them glow. Like playing a game of *Cranium.* You just smile and clap and ask them to do it again. Hooray! Bravo! Uno Mas! *Are you enabling people to do what they do best?*

18. **Tell people why.** Never assume anyone knows your reasoning for doing anything. So, don't DEFEND yourself; explain yourself. Make your motivations and intentions crystal clear. When you tell people why, they're more likely to (1) believe you, (2) understand you, and (3) respond TO you. *Are you constantly making people aware of your Why?*

19. **Train people's eyes.** Ever tried to show someone how to stare at a Magic Eye poster? You probably said something like, "Just relax your eyes, soften your gaze and don't look at anything particular." The same process goes for life. When you're with someone, explain your thinking process out loud as you observe. Let them hear how you process your visuals. Explain your inner monologue. Let them hear how you ask yourself questions. *Whose eyes are YOU training?*

20. **Unlock people's brilliance.** First, you've got to trust that people inherently possess brilliance, buried deep beneath the surface. Second, you've got to be willing to divorce your ego, ask more questions, grow bigger ears and shut up quicker. Third, you've got to let THEM figure it out – that is, let THEM say it, know it, do it, BE it – by their own merit. Finally, you've got to constantly reinforce people's brilliance by reminding them what a Smokin' Hot Piece of Brain Candy they really are. These four keys, when practiced regularly, will unlock the door to people's brilliance. *How can you make this person look and feel smarter?*

REMEMBER: You can choose to influence people through (1) what you believe, (2) what you say, (3) what you do, or, best of all, (4) *who you are.*

Do that, and I promise that people will want to sit in your radius.

HELLO
MY NAME IS CHAPTER,

five

How do people experience you?

Think about the first time you heard your own voice on tape.
Odds are, your initial reaction was, "Is THAT what I really sound like?"

Now think about the first time you watched yourself on video.
Odds are, your initial reaction was, "Is THAT what I really look like?"

Don't worry. That's a pretty normal response.

See, most of us – when given an honest, accurate reflection of the way we present ourselves to the others – are startled by our own lack of self-awareness. We can't believe that's actually us. And not just on audio and video. For example, think about some of these other silent dialogues:

- "Did I really say that?"
- "Is that really the way I came off?"
- "I didn't realize I was making you feel that way."
- "I had no idea that's what people thought of me…"

Ever said one of those to yourself before?

I know I have. Probably once this week already. And I'd be willing to bet that most people have too.

These kinds of perceptions exist in your "Blind Spot." Cognitive psychologists Joseph Luft and Harry Ingham defined this term in 1955 as, "Aspects of ourselves that others see, but we are not aware of."

SO, HERE'S THE CHALLENGE: Make a concerted effort to unalienate yourself from your truth.

Because too many of us – and even I'm guilty of this on occasion – demonstrate a complete and utter unwillingness to understand: (1) How other people experience us, and (2) How other people experience *themselves* in relation to us.

And the danger of this pattern of behavior is that it prevents people from asking questions of, listening to, learning from and getting to know you.

Not good.

Maybe it's time to run honest self-appraisal.
Maybe it's time to get bitten by the bug of self-awareness.

Or, as Dilbert cartoonist Scott Adams said, "Awareness means recognizing your illusions for what they are."

Because, as you learned earlier, the only judgment people can make – the only impression their unconscious mind can form – is how interacting with you makes them FEEL.

And ultimately, it doesn't matter what YOU think, it matters what THEY remember.

So, I'm challenging you to (honestly) ask yourself **two critical questions**:

 1. How do people experience you?
 2. How do people experience themselves when they're with you?

Take some time this week to physically write out your answers to those questions. Reflect on whether your inner experience matches how others experience you. This will serve as the perfect starting point in the development of your newfound self-awareness.

Then, once you've taken enough self-stock, the next step will be actually OPENING yourself to the reality of how your behavior affects the people around you.

That's the cool part of starting down the rewarding path of self-awareness. Once you know your patterns – once you know how others experience you – you'll start to see the following positive changes in your world:

- You gain the power to grow.
- You represent yourself better to others.
- You become safer for others to be around.
- You become someone others could tell anything.
- You become perceived as listenable and askable.
- You make a stronger emotional impact on others.
- You encourage a more positive perception of yourself.
- You deepen your ability to consider and weigh alternatives.
- You give others the knowledge they need to love you more.
- You meet WITH, speak TO and touch people where they are.
- You hold yourself accountable for your contributions to your encounters.
- You find out where you suck, that way you can close the perception gaps between you and those you serve.

Let's explore a list of strategies for making these changes a reality:

1. Assure you don't leave people feeling unheard. Towards the end of your interaction, it might be helpful to ask summary or clarification questions like:

- Is there anything else?
- What questions have I not answered yet?
- What questions did I not ask that you were hoping I'd ask?

Also, let people know that if they think of another question in the next day or two that didn't come up during the conversation, they can reach out to you. Even a follow up email a day or two later wouldn't be a bad idea. As long as the impression is that you're curious for clarity and not an overwhelming micromanager.

2. Be aware of the weight you have on people. A common mistake made by unapproachable leaders is forgetting to regularly share what they're thinking and feeling. This confusion over where the leader stands causes stress in their followers. After all, when people never know what's on your mind, it drives them crazy. And ultimately, the weight you have on them will become so heavy that your unpredictability will create apprehension in their process of approaching you.

What's more, let's talk about the peril of passion. Sure, passion is beautiful because it's enthusiastic and contagious. But be careful. Part of being an approachable leader is cultivating an awareness of how your energy affects others. Take a campfire, for example. Yes, it provides warmth. Yes, it provides inspiration. Yes, it provides heat to cook your s'mores. But it can also burn you (and others) pretty good. Make sure your intensity doesn't wear people out. Beware of becoming someone who makes other people tired just by looking at you.

3. Create the space people need to exert their distinctiveness. Think about the type of person you would have to become to make even the shyest people willing to open up around you. Would that mean uncovering parts of your own life are you not giving yourself permission to live creatively? Absolutely. So, consider the following *Permission Questions* as a test of how well you execute this principle:

- Are you granting others space to BE?
- What questions are people afraid to ask you?
- Are you giving people permission to talk to you?
- What feelings are you not allowing people to have?
- What feelings are you not giving people space to feel?
- How are you resisting or suppressing the creativity of others?
- Are you giving people permission to feel playful around you?
- Are you giving people permission to make their own choices?
- When was the last time someone told you something they hadn't told anyone else?
- What parts of others' lives are you not giving them permission to live creatively?
- What type of person would you have to become to make even the shyest people willing to open up around you?

The secret is finding a safe space to understand people's unique reality; then giving them permission to reveal it to you. And that might be as simple as pausing; then listening for greatness to show up in each person.

4. Don't overwhelm people with your knowledge. In *Rules of Thumb*, Alan Webber identifies two types of leaders: The ones who compliment other people they work with for their ideas, and the one who use their incredible brainpower to point out the flaws in others' thinking and shoot down their ideas.

Hopefully, you're the former: Someone who shares knowledge without showcasing it; someone who presents ideas without hurling them. Try this: If you have a lot of ideas to convey, chunk them down into small clusters. By spacing ideas effectively, they're easier to digest. Otherwise people feel intimidated by a barrage of knowledge, which reduces receptivity.

5. Don't ignore signs of discomfort in others. That means refraining from telling a lot of insignificant, endless stories that have zero relevance to anyone. This is not only uncomfortable, but also annoying. And it leaves a perception of vanity – not value – in the minds of others. And yet, countless leaders practice this without invitation and it drives others up the wall. So consumed with telling their story, they pay little or no attention to people's irritation, impatience or disgust. Scott Adams said it best in *Dogbert's Top Secret Management Handbook,* "Be obliged to stop rambling if your listener shows signs of starvation, coma or rigor mortis."

6. Help people become the best version of themselves. Your challenge is to assist people in identifying their states of peak performance. Here are a few "best questions" to try out:

- What is present when you're at your BEST?
- What about the situation brought out the BEST in you?
- You, yourself, are at your BEST when you're acting HOW?
- When have you felt that your actions spoke for the BEST in who you are?
- What behaviors are preventing you from making progress towards becoming the BEST version of yourself?

The cool part is, questions like these help people bring to the surface a slice of their core selfhood that they've encountered before. And when they experience themselves in such a beautiful light, it leaves a permanent imprint on their spirit. All because instead of IN-forming people, you made the choice to FORM people. Which allowed them to walk away from the conversation feeling more confident in their truth.

7. Identify and disarm silent dialogues. *Assumptions. Annoyances. Preoccupations. Concerns. Questions.* This is just a sampling of the communication barriers floating around in people's heads. See, the big question people are asking themselves (as they experience you) is, "Is this person the same on the inside as he seems on the outside?"

For your sake, I hope the answer is yes. In Parker Palmer's fantastic book, *A Hidden Wholeness,* he addresses this perception gap:

"When the answer to that question is yes, we relax. We believe that we are in the presence of integrity and feel secure enough to invest ourselves in the relationship. When the answer to that question is no, we go on high alert. Not knowing who or what are dealing with and feeling unsafe, we hunker down into a psychological foxhole and withhold the investment of our energy, commitment and gifts."

8. Learn to spy on yourself more often. Just to see how you're doing. Checkin' yourself out. Observing various situations and experiences behind that internal pane of two-way glass and taking copious notes. (It's become kind of a hobby of mine.)

But it's not easy. Part of this process comes from your ability to detach, disassociate and sort of "get out of yourself" for a while, looking inward at your own behavior. One practice I've found to be successful is self-questioning. Gently poking your inner landscape with an inquiry or two about what's going on in the now. Try these:

- Is it my place to fix this?
- How am I making decisions?
- Is this a thought or an impulse?
- If I were me, what would I do in this situation?
- In what ways am I reacting, instead of responding?
- What are the consequences of the choice I'm making?
- Would I want to become known for what I'm about to do?
- What values of this person might I have violated, and how is that resulting in him shutting down communication?

The goal is to create a sense of awareness in which your attention is focused on your own behavior, 100% in the moment, watching yourself as if you were the star of a mystery movie.

9. Paint a picture of what happens when people are marinated in your world. This can be accomplished by considering the communication climate you create around you. Noticing how you come off. Understanding what people get when they get you. Discovering how most people feel when they're around you. And, by deciding how you want people to describe the experience of interacting with you.

Here are a few additional self-assessment questions to assist you in this discovery process:

- What do people hear when they listen to what you do?
- Is communicating with you a relaxing or stressful experience?
- When interacting with you, what is this person's immediate physical experience?
- When you meet people, is your first thought about what they think of you or how you can make them more comfortable?

Additionally: Watch people's physiology. Step outside yourself and honestly observe the way they're reacting to you. And listen to the *exact words* people use when they introduce or describe you to someone new.

Also (on the non-conversational level) Google Alerts are a GREAT tool for understanding how people experience you AND themselves in relation TO you. Register alerts on your name, company name, nickname, tagline, Twitter ID, websites or anything else related to your reputation, identity and perception – online and offline.

Then: Listen, listen and listen. Thank people for their feedback. Keep a log. It's great insight into what happens when people are marinated in your world.

10. Recognize, embrace and respond to the value others place on you. That's the constant challenge of proactive approachability: Understanding what "time with you" is (really) worth to other people. Because if you don't recognize this currency, you may never think to offer yourself as much, or at all, to those who need you.

Then others might think, "I hate to take up his time when so many people want time with him." Don't assume that if people want to be with you they'll just say so. If you do, you will seldom take the first step and ask for anyone's time. And as a result, you'll miss out on encounters with some VERY cool people.

People are waiting for YOU to initiate the next meeting. Be proactive. Offer yourself more consciously, actively and directly to them. If you can practice this strategy, people will appreciate your recognition of the perceived value they place on you.

To conclude this module, here's an exercise:

PICTURE THIS: Somebody just finishes interacting with you. Phone, email, in person, Twitter, whatever. And this person could be a customer, coworker, colleague, manager or employee.

Five minutes later, she walks into the bathroom with her best friend. And she starts telling her friend all about how she experienced you, AND how she experienced herself when she was with you. From five minutes ago.

Now, here's the twist: During this conversation, the only other person in the bathroom is YOU. Silently crouching on the toilet, eavesdropping on these two people talking about ... YOU.

And so, the two final questions I want you to honestly ask yourself are:

What would they say about you?
How surprised would you be?

Is there a gap between your onstage performance and backstage reality?

Let me ask ya this:

1. Are the stories people tell about you the same stories you tell about yourself?
2. What's the gap between how you want to be seen and how others experience you now?
3. And how does that gap between your onstage performance and your backstage reality affect the daily lives of the people you serve?

Frustrated by your own answers?

That's not entirely surprising. As Stanley Bing explained in *Zen and the Art of Managing Up,* "The distance between what you believe you are and the actual reality of your true nature will make you angry."

Here are few suggestions for narrowing that gap:

1. **Allow your truthful self-expression to inspire others to do (and BE) the same.** Because when you applaud the gifts of YOU, you are able to applaud the gifts of those around you.

2. **Let people experience that they can change your mind.** Sometimes we're too close to the parts of ourselves that drive other people crazy. As Robert

Sutton suggests in *The No Asshole Rule*, "Stop doing things that provoke people who don't know you well to mislabel you as a jerk."

3. **Listen careful to how people describe the way they experience OTHER people.** Then, ask yourself how well – or how poorly – you're performing in those same areas. Use others' behaviors as mirrors to reflect your own image back to yourself. Then, physically write them out, identify their positive attributes and then begin to embody them in your own life.

4. **Share comments that honor the other person's unique feelings, thoughts and emotions.** However you respond, just make sure there's an undercurrent that communicates, "This is how I truly feel about what you've just offered me."

5. **Stay sensitive to this person's immediate experience of you.** People rarely forget how you treated them the last time. Therefore: Everything is a performance, everything matters and everybody is watching. Which isn't terribly difficult if the character you're playing is yourself. Therefore: Being approachable isn't enough. You need to be PERCEIVED AS and REMEMBERED AS being approachable as well.

... have conversations that change people.

Dixie Gillaspie, owner of Pure Synchrony, is a colleague of mine that I refuse to have lunch with unless I bring my notebook. She's just THAT thought provoking. And, every time we get together, her questions, feedback, comments and ideas always create movement in my mind.

She's an approachable leader because her conversations change people. Here are four ways you can start LIVING this attribute today:

1. **Ask one killer question.** Identify ONE powerful, penetrating question that nobody else asks but you. Then ask it to everyone you meet. My question is, "If everyone did exactly what you said, what would the world look like?"

2. **Offer intentional contraries.** When someone poses an idea, reverse it and throw it back at him. Just to see his response. For example, I recently said to one of my coaching clients, "Well, Steve, in addition to thinking about what you want your life to look like, also ask yourself, 'What do you want your life NOT to look like?'"

3. **Keep a record.** Any time one of your employees, members (or someone in your circle of influence) tells you that your recent conversation with them was life changing, make a note. Keep each of these incidents in a journal. Extract the specific reasons WHY each conversation created movement in that person's mind. Find out where the rock created the ripple, and then go throw some more rocks.

4. **Choose to attend differently to this person.** Not "type." Not "deal with." Not "tolerate." Not "manipulate." Attend. This word comes from the French *atendre*, which means, "to direct one's mind or energies." Wow. Sounds so much friendlier. More approachable. More relaxing. Less judgmental and suspicious, too. Try this: Dance in the moment. Ask yourself how you could attend differently to this person. Stop putting people in predictable little boxes with handy little labels that read, "introvert" or "right brained" or "potential serial killer." Get to know people for who they really are; not what others have haphazardly labeled them as. You never know. They might turn out to be pretty cool after all. Serial killers have feelings too, you know.

LET ME ASK YA THIS: How are people changed after having a conversation with you?

HELLO
MY NAME IS CHAPTER,

seven

How are you making communication a relaxing experience?

My friend Arthur is pretty chill.
Whenever we hang out, our time together is relaxing.
Which (also) makes our time together enjoyable and productive.
You know, like you want to skip your next appointment and just keep talking all morning.

My friend Sandi is quite scatterbrained.
Whenever we hang out, our time together is fairly tense.
Which (also) makes our time together frustrating and inefficient.
You know, like you want to hurry up and finish the conversation so you can go in the bathroom and do a few deep breathing exercises.

Two different people, two different communication experiences. *Which one are YOU? Which one do you WANT to be? Which one do your customers PERCEIVE you as being?*

Hopefully, you're more like Arthur.

HERE'S THE SECRET: When you relax, you win. When you relax, others win. Period.

Take it from someone who didn't (used to) know how to relax.

Take it from someone who was hospitalized three times in six months because he wasn't relaxing enough.

Take it from someone who writes books about being approachable and used to be SO tense all the time ... *that he felt like a walking contradiction.*

(That's me, by the way.)

The challenge is figuring out how to make communication a relaxing experience *based on your own personal style*. Because there's no ONE WAY to do it.

Today we're going to explore eight practices that will put you – and, therefore, others – at ease. Also, along with each example, I've included a few "Sticky Note Suggestions." You might consider posting these mantras and questions in visible location as reminders to make communication a relaxing experience.

1. **Start with yourself.** Relaxation is contagious. The best way to put others at ease is to be at ease yourself. So, practice relaxing more. Especially outside of the interpersonal context. My first suggestion is to incorporate a daily routine of mind/body/spirit practice. Yoga, meditation, deep breathing, guided imagery, journaling or self-hypnosis – whatever works for you. This will lay a general foundation of calmness that will carry over to ALL your daily activities. *And people will notice the difference.* Personally, I never miss a day.

    Secondly, prepare yourself to listen. Before going on a conference call, giving a presentation, attending networking events, running staff meetings or any other form of person-to-person contact, first take some time for yourself. Consult your materials. Do a few breathing exercises at your desk or in your car. Recite positive affirmations. Anything that lays a foundation of confidence and preparation.

    STICKY NOTE REMINDER: Try questions like, "Are you relaxed?" "Did you meditate today?" and "**REMEMBER:** YOU come first" to keep you focused on the most important person in the world.

2. **Find excuses to smile.** Smiles are among the easiest, quickest and most effective behaviors for putting someone at ease. A great suggestion is to smile for TEN SECONDS every time you walk into a room. Also, try playing the "Let's See What I Can Find in This Room to Make Me Smile" game. Look around. See if you can spot some kids. That usually works. Or someone with a wacky haircut. Also effective. Whatever gets those pearly whites to show. Cheesy? *Maybe.* Effective? *Absolutely.*

STICKY NOTE REMINDER: Post a favorite movie line, picture or quotation that's guaranteed to make you smile when you look at it. Anything from *Spaceballs* works.

3. **Monopolize the listening.** Next time you meet someone at a networking event, see how long you can go without talking. Or interrupting. Or inserting your clever little jokes or witty comments. Strive to listen twice as much as you talk. Ask a few thought provoking questions, then sit back and let your ears grow. Participate, but don't dominate. Dance in the moment and facilitate the exploration of the other person's experience.

STICKY NOTE SUGGESTION: Try posting, "L-I-S-T-E-N = S-I-L-E-N-T," "Two Ears, One Mouth," or "Ask, don't tell" around your office.

4. **Remember ... to pause.** Pausing creates space, space enables clarity, and clarity eases the mind. Examples: Remember to pause before you give an answer, after you ask a question, when someone else is on a roll, or after powerful insights. Then, allow people's words and ideas to profoundly penetrate you, as well as allowing YOUR words to profoundly penetrate others.

STICKY NOTE REMINDER: Draw the "pause" symbol from your remote control and stick it on the edge of your computer screen.

5. **Remember to breathe.** Speaking of pausing. When you consciously take deep, slow breaths, your heart rate and blood pressure lower. Fresh oxygen, fresh life, flows through your body. *Ahhh...!* But what's amazing is how often we forget to breathe. Especially when we're communicating with someone. We get so involved, so excited, so engaged, that we lose sight of the most important thing in the world.

REMEMBER: Breath is life. This is something you learn when you wake up at 7 AM on a Saturday morning because your left lung collapsed and now you have to spend the next week of your life sitting in a bed at Missouri Baptist Hospital whacked out on morphine with a tube in your chest. Hypothetically, of course.

STICKY NOTE REMINDER: Post the question "How's your breathing?" on your phone.

6. **Love the silence.** Something that ISN'T relaxing is when people keep talking, just for the sake of talking. They break the silence, just to fill the space. They ask more and more questions, but only because nobody's

spoken for a few minutes. Be careful of this trap, as it is easy to fall into. Learn to accept silence as a normal, beautiful and essential part of your conversations.

REMEMBER: Just because someone isn't speaking doesn't mean they're not thinking. Embrace the silence. Sometimes it's better than talking. In the words of bluegrass beauty Allison Krauss, "You say it best when you say nothing at all."

STICKY NOTE REMINDER: Write the words, "Silence is beautiful" or "Love the silence" and post it in your office.

7. **Humor relaxes people.** So, just be funny! Early and often. Humor lubricates your message and allows people to digest (and remember) it easily. Now, that doesn't mean, "make jokes." That doesn't mean turn your meeting into a standup routine. And that doesn't mean bounce around the room like Ace Ventura. *That means allow your natural humor to shine.*

And if you're saying to yourself, "Yeah, but I'm just not funny…" Wrong. You're hilarious. Everyone is. You just haven't pinpointed your Humor Sources yet. Think about the ten sources of constant humor in your life. Kids? Pets? Ex-Husbands? Write them down. Under each category, brainstorm three short stories that personify that humor. Keep the list handy. Rehearse them if you have to. Then, refer to it often. You'll be good to go.

STICKY NOTE REMINDER: Ask yourself, "Are they laughing?"

REMEMBER: Relaxing = Enjoyable and productive. Tense = Frustrating and efficient.

The choice is yours.

Ultimately, you DON'T want to be the type of person that stresses other people out just by being around you. Because what *might* eventually happen is, those people WON'T want to be around you anymore.

HELLO
MY NAME IS CHAPTER,

eight

Are you the most inspirational person you know?

The word "inspire" derives from the Latin *inspiraire*, which means, "to breathe into."

So, I'm curious: *As a leader, what are YOU breathing into people?*

Hope? Passion? Confidence? Garlic?

I know. Kind of tough question. And if you can't think of your answer right away, don't sweat it.

WHAT you breathe into people isn't as important as THAT you breathe into people.

HERE'S THE REALITY: Being an inspirational person is combination of three elements…

1. The person you've become.
2. How people experience you.
3. How people experience themselves in relation TO you.

Unfortunately – despite your best efforts – you CAN'T inspire everyone you encounter.

Some people just aren't inspirable.

No matter how hard you work to raise their receptivity.
No matter how many positive quotations you write on their dry erase board.

Not everyone wants (or is ready to) be inspired.

And that's fine. Your life's work shouldn't to inspire people.

Rather, your mission is to identify and embody the attributes of inspirational people.

That's the only way to increase the probability that other people will become inspired.

Here's a list of strategies for becoming the most inspirational person you know:

1. **Create an avenue for others to benefit from your unique gifts.** Maybe it's via your blog. Maybe it's out in the community. Maybe it's on the radio. Maybe it's in the local newspaper. The point is: We've all been given unique gifts. And our sole assignment during the short time we spend on this Earth is to return the favor by regifting to make the world more beautiful.

   And the best part is, our usefulness isn't just a form of worship – it's also a form inspiration. Think about it: Do you know anyone with incredible gifts (who SHARES those gifts regularly) that ISN'T inspiring?

   So, your challenge is to clarify your contribution. To leave this cosmic campsite called life better than the way you found it. To validate your existence by making passion palpable. And to take whatever unique gift you've been given and re-gift it by exploiting it in the service of others. Interestingly, the word "contribute" comes from the Latin, *contributus*, which means, "to bring together." *What are you bringing together? What were you made to make?*

2. **Don't start doing something special – STOP doing something normal.** Instead of immediately shooting down every suggestion people offer with an objection that proves how smart you are, just stop. Breathe. Then, leverage that opportunity as a teachable moment. As my fried "Genuine" Chris Johnson says, "Most people have raging impulses to interrupt one another. Instead, show some restraint. Suppress conversational tension by waiting for your turn to share poignant insights."

   Be not seduced by the dark side. Curb the craving to spew a steady stream self-glorifying wisdom that's inherently impressive and interesting, yet obviously irrelevant and inapplicable. *What could you do in this situation that would be the polar opposite of everybody else?*

3. **Help people fall in love with themselves.** First, by falling in love with YOUR self. This allows people to see firsthand what it's like when someone

honors their Truth. And that experience is inspiring because it grants people permission to do (and BE) the same. Also, remember that being an inspirational person is about how people experience themselves when they're with you – AND when they walk away from you. So, make them feel better off having communicated with you. Pinpoint the beauty that they're too close to themselves to taste. That's what inspiration is: Breathing into people a reflection of their awesomeness. *What would happen if everyone who walked away from you was inspired to lead with her truth more frequently?*

4. **Help surprising thinking emerge around you.** It happened halfway through a recent business coaching session. My client, Patrick, just sort of stopped mid-sentence, laughed to himself and confessed, "You know Scott, I didn't realize how much I sucked until you told me!" We actually had a good laugh about it. And, I WILL say, that although my coaching style has never been to "give people a breakdown so they can achieve a breakthrough," Patrick's comment WAS a valuable insight.

He demonstrated that he was inspired share his vulnerability. Which was pretty cool. And so, I reassured him that he wasn't dumb, and that my job wasn't to make him FEEL dumb. Rather, as his coach, my job was to disturb him into action. And the cool part is, ever since I witnessed Patrick's epiphany while he experienced HIMSELF in relation to me; I've now been able to spur my other clients into action using similar self-inspiring approaches. *Are you willing to ante up first and disclosure your vulnerability so other people will feel inspired to reciprocate?*

5. **Learn by what you have LIVED, then teach people.** Inspirational people know that *orthopraxy* (the right practices) is exponentially more powerful that *orthodoxy* (the right beliefs). After all: People aren't inspired by what they HEAR you SAY consistently. People only inspired by what they SEE you DO consistently.

Being an inspirational person means that instead of practicing what you preach, you're preaching what you practice. In the words of my inspiring friend/mentor Jim Henderson: "Action changes everything. We need to major in practices and minor in principles. Practices are attitudes that translate directly into actions."

If you want to be an inspiration, try this: Do something first, THEN tell people about. Do something first, THEN tell people what you learned. Do something first, THEN challenge people to do the same. *Is the message you're preaching the dominant reality of your life?*

6. **Make certain people regularly experience you in your element.** Windsurfing. Baking. Fixing cars. Solving math problems. Riding horses. Being a Mom. Selling hot dogs to drunken Cardinal fans at the Busch Stadium. Whatever. Pinpoint your natural state of magnificence, and then stay there for as long as you can. It doesn't matter what you're amazing at.

When people get the chance to see you being you, doing what you do best, it will always be inspirational. And it will be impossible for them to escape your awesomeness. So, seek out situations that vividly reveal your passions, and then make sure LOTS of people are watching. *How are you constantly expanding your platform on which to display your gifts?*

7. **Pepper in ordinariness.** One of the problems with so-called "inspirational" people is that they're completely unrelatable. No disrespect to Oprah, but come on. Nobody can relate to her. I don't care how "regular" she claims to be on her show. Oprah is a cyborg from planet Zoltar, and she does not live in a world of reality

Unless you regularly exert your ordinariness, people wall have a hard time spotting your humanity. There must be a balance between being admirable; yet relatable. Not being utterly boring; yet not being terminally unique. *How well do you merge ordinariness with remarkability?*

8. **Produce or arouse a feeling.** This is another official definition of the word "inspire." Take George Carlin, for example. As a writer, performer and philosopher, he has always been an inspiration to me because of his ability to arouse feelings in people. Shortly after he passed away in 2008, I watched an old interview between him and the (then) young Jon Stewart. When asked about his childhood education, Carlin replied with probably the most powerful lesson I've ever heard him share:

"When I was in school I got all A's: I got their attention, their approval, their admiration and their applause." Holy crap. Can you imagine how many people you could inspire if YOU got all A's? *Who do you have to become to earn instant applause from more people?*

9. **Put a stake in the ground and guard it fiercely.** Start by precisely defining the values that have the most power in your heart. Write them down on a small laminated card. Keep it in your wallet at all times. Although not everyone will agree with you, your solid stance will challenge people to think about their own stake in the ground. *What issue would you protest publicly? What are you a crusader of?*

10. **Screw up more.** Flawless execution doesn't exist. Make mistakes, make them early and make them quick. Then keep moving. Doing so inspires people to share their own flawed ideas, thoughts and concerns. Why? *Because you've PROVEN to them that you support failure.* And it is only when you're willing to surrender to your own imperfect humanity that people lower their guard and start to trust you more. *Make any mistakes today?*

11. **See connections nobody sees.** "Damn! I wish I'd thought of that!" If anyone's ever said this to you before, congratulations. You're on the right track to becoming inspirational. This common exclamation is rooted in excitement, admiration and maybe even a little envy. And people usually say it when they're exposed to something that anybody could have done, but only one person actually did.

    As my inspirational colleague Andy Sernovitz of www.damniwish.com says, "It's not the result of good luck or wacky stunts. It's a planned, well-executed strategy to earn the respect of your customers and get them talking about you. It's the philosophy that treating people well — wowing them — is a long-term, sustainable growth strategy." *Who wants to grow up and become the next YOU?*

12. **Share who inspired YOU.** If you want to be inspirational, you have to start by being inspired yourself. "Inspirational people make staying inspired part of their purpose in life," says Dixie Gillaspie, my inspiring coach. "And, it's not only about being inspired yourself, but also willing to unstintingly share WHAT inspired you. Which means you have to translate and distill what you've learned so others easily internalize it." *Who inspired you? How are you continuously inviting inspiration into your life?*

13. **Show how far you've come.** Then, show people how far THEY'VE come. This will challenge them to think about the person they've become, and what it took for them to get there. This will allow them to inspire themselves. Especially when you remind people that nobody can take away what they've become. *What have you become?*

14. **Stick yourself out there.** Leaders ante up first. They take the first step to inspire others to do the same. So, think of five people that inspire you. On a scale of 1-10, how willing to risk were those people? My guess: Very. Because that's what inspirational people do – they stick themselves out there.

    In the words of my inspiring colleague, David Garland, producer of <u>The Rise to The Top</u> television show, "Inspiration correlates with risk. Those that take (some sort of) risk are perceived as inspirational because they're just regular people who did something remarkable."

That's the cool part. We're not just talking about *physical risk* like bungee jumping or wearing a Cowboys jersey to an Eagles game. Sticking yourself out there is an emotional risk. It's about walking your truth in a world of mostly fiction. And that's what inspires people to want to walk THEIR Truth as well. *What dream in you (that could inspire others) would cause you deep regret if you never took the risk to go for it?*

15. **Take massive action.** Action is the hallmark of inspiration. Period. It doesn't matter what you believe. Or intend. Or even what you say. Believing is overrated. Intending is useless. Talking is worthless. *Doing,* on the other hand, isn't. It never has been. Action is, always has been – and always will be – inspirational. And your challenge is to continuously TAKE massive action. Every day. Constantly shoveling coal into your engine of inspiration.

Inspirational people make realities out of things most people only dream of doing. And it doesn't require genius. Or lots of money. Or years and years of study. It takes jeuvos. Chutzpah. Guts. Execution. Follow through. Stick-to-it-ive-ness.

Suffering from a deficiency in those areas? No problem. Go read The Cult of Done Manifesto. That'll get your butt in gear. Don't wait for overwhelming evidence before trusting yourself. Just go. Plunge into the vortex of action. *What can you do in the first half of today to demonstrate focus and unstoppable action?*

REMEMBER: You can't inspire everyone you encounter.

All you can do is actively make yourself into a more inspirational person.

What are YOU breathing into people?

... vortex you in.

My high school English teacher, mentor and close friend, William Jenkins, is the consummate example of approachability. He's the kind of guy whose presence you value SO much, that when you're with him, simply "absorbing who he is" is enough.

Whether you've taken his class at Parkway North, attended his church in Troy, MO; read any of his gazillion books or enjoyed his conversation, one thing's for sure: You're there to listen. You're there to take notes. You're there to observe Bill being Bill. As his students like to call it, "We've enrolled in The Jenkins Experience.".

Here are four ways you can start LIVING this attribute today:

1. **Ask character questions.** Honestly assess: "Are you spending time increasing your talent or increasing your character?" "Have you made it a practice to take full responsibility for your character?" and "What are you biggest character flaws?"

2. **Don't take yourself too seriously.** Sure, you can take your work and your life and your health and your family seriously. But not yourself. Try a little self-deprecating humor once in a while. It grounds you and puts people at ease.

3. **Behavior is the broadcaster of attitude.** Your behavior will have a very hard time telling a lie. There are simply too many people watching. You think people are listening to your words, thoughts and attitudes? Nope. Read all the Norman Vincent Peale books you want, but if you're punching holes your cubicle wall because the shite economy lowered sales by 30%, your attitude clearly sucks.

   Here's an idea: Ask yourself questions like, "Is how I'm behaving right now consistent with the attitude I strive to maintain?" and "What behaviors are preventing me from making progress towards becoming the best version of myself?" Identify the disconnect. Then stop what you're doing immediately, before anyone else tunes into the frequency of your inconsistency.

4. **Give people permission to comfortably, confidently and consistently BE their true selves.** The easiest way to do that is to comfortably, confidently and consistently be YOUR true self first. When you know your boundaries, you know who you are. When you know who you are, you feel more confident. When you feel more confident, you aren't threatened by other people's differences. When you aren't threatened by other people's differences, you do not threaten them. When people aren't threatened by each other, they accept each other. When people accept each other, the rules change. Cool.

LET ME ASK YA THIS: Who wants to sit in your radius?

HELLO
MY NAME IS CHAPTER,

nine

How are you leaving a permanent imprint on people?

Emotion is the final arbiter of truth.

Which means you have a choice: Will people feel diminished, unaffected, or enlarged after their encounters with you?

TRY THIS: Constantly ask yourself the question, "What new world could I open up for this person?"

Because all it takes is one powerful insight, one thought-provoking question or one engaging conversation to send someone off to the races.

To get her hamster wheel spinning furiously. To change her thinking FOR-ever.

It's all in the delivery, too. For example, the seven words that left a permanent imprint on me were "Writing is the basis of all wealth." (Thanks, Jeffrey Gitomer.)

Now, you can read those words on paper, but it doesn't have the same effect. So, whenever I pass along that particular nugget to one of my coaching clients, here's what I do, and I challenge you to do the same in order to leave an imprint on people:

1. **Prepare the person to receive.** Paired with direct eye contact, I'll say, "Erin, I want you to listen very closely to what I'm about to tell you…"

2. **Punctuate with a five-second pause.** After I say, "Writing is the basis of all wealth," I shut up and stare. This allows my words to profoundly penetrate and, hopefully, disturb her.

3. **Say it again.** Repetition reemphasizes importance.

4. **Make it tangible.** I then write the sentence down on a little piece of paper and physically hand it to her, ask her to write it down herself, or email her later that day as a reminder.

5. **Pound it in.** Through her brain, past her heart and down to her soul. And I do this by constantly repeating those words over and over: "Remember what we talked about Erin: Writing is the basis of all wealth."

That's how you alter people's pulses.
That's how you leave a permanent imprint on them.

LET ME ASK YA THIS: *What do people get from communicating with you? How are they changed after having a conversation with you? And do they feel diminished, unaffected, or enlarged after their encounters with you?*

HELLO
MY NAME IS CHAPTER,

ten

How are people changed after having a conversation with you?

Everyone has peeps.

No, not those cute little marshmallow birds you buy on Easter and stick in the microwave until they explode.

I'm talking about your PEOPLE.

Employees. Clients. Guests. Fans. Readers. Listeners. Viewers. Attendees. Colleagues. Members. Congregants. Friends. Students. Children.

You know, your peeps. Your constituency. Those you serve on a daily basis.

And when it comes to your interactions with these people, there's a fundamental question that has to be asked:

How are people changed after having a conversation with you?

Too many leaders – and, we're ALL leaders, by the way – would not be able to answer this question effectively.

Take my old boss, for example. When I first launched my publishing/consulting company, I used to valet ~~crash~~ park cars nights and weekends at a local hotel to make ends meet. David, the colossal putz known as my boss, was the kind of guy who made you walk away from a conversation saying to yourself, "You know, maybe committing suicide by drinking an entire bottle of Armor All isn't just a bad option after all…"

Not exactly the "change after a conversation" I was looking for.

HERE'S THE GOOD NEWS: As a leader, you can exert (some) degree of control over the outcomes of your interactions.

We're going to explore three practices to make sure your peeps are positively changed after having a conversation with you.

1. **Make people better off having communicated with you.** You can do so by pointing out what people are too close to themselves to hear. This helps people listen to the loudest message their lives are screaming. A few *Phrases That Payses* might include: "As I silently listened to you, I heard some messages that you yourself couldn't hear..." and "Mary, here's what I heard emerging out of everything you shared..."

    When you practice this, people don't just LIKE themselves when they're with you; they LOVE themselves when they walk away from you. And the best part is (as my friend Dixie likes to remind me), "When people are in love with themselves, they will love whoever made them feel that way. And we do anything for the people we love." *How do you leave people?*

2. **Make time spent with you seem longer.** Look, I know you're busy. So, whether you're interacting with employees, clients, guests, attendees, colleagues, members, congregants, friends and students – even your own kids – the secret is to make their (limited) time with you seem longer. Here's how:

    SIT DOWN. In the book *Healing Words*, a 2003 study from Columbia University reported that doctors who physically sat down during their consultations were perceived by patients as being in the room THREE TIMES longer than the doctors who stood up. *Wow.*

    WATCH YOUR EYES. Avoid any movement that seems like you are checking on how much time has passed. No matter how busy you are. No matter how badly you have to pee. Be aware of how often your eyes avert from the speaker and scan clocks, phones, pagers or computer screens. People WILL notice. If you absolutely HAVE to look, do it discreetly or wait until the other person isn't watching. *D'oh!*

    AVOID THE WORD "ONLY." In Parker Palmer's book, A Hidden Wholeness, he explains, "Only is a negative presumption. By simply saying, 'Come in, I have ten minutes,' versus, 'Come in, I ONLY have ten minutes," you are perceived as someone who gives others enough time."

Otherwise there will be a perpetual undercurrent of resentment. And that tension will give people the impression that your time is more valuable than theirs. Yikes.

REMEMBER: Approachability is about the openness and attractiveness of your physical space as a function of your language, behaviors and environment. *What would happen to your reputation as a leader if you became known as someone who made time for everyone?*

3. **Compliment people's being, not doing.** Scrap those cheesy, ass-kissing techniques of complimenting people's clothes or hairstyles. The interpersonal impact of such compliments is directly proportionate to the level of thought required to deliver them: NONE. Instead, ask yourself, "What could I say to honor this person's uniqueness?" "What attributes of her core self do I admire?" and "What facets of his personhood are most attractive?"

Suggestion: For the love of God, don't place your cell phone on the table while you're having a face-to-face conversation. Don't even look at it. All that signals to people is, "I might be receiving a call from someone who is more important than you." *Do you really think complimenting her new hairstyle is REALLY going to make her want to follow you?*

REMEMBER: Part of being an approachable leader depends on how people feel when they walk away from you.

The choice is yours.

Your peeps are waiting.

HELLO
MY NAME IS CHAPTER,

eleven

Are you leading from the heart or the handbook?

The formula for approachable leadership is simple:

Heart Over Handbook – Soul Over Script.

That means you need to be CONSISTENT.
Because consistency is far better than rare moments of greatness.

That means you need to maintain INTEGRITY.
Because people are listening to the sound of your actions.

That means you need to articulate your BOUNDARIES.
Because if you don't set healthy boundaries for yourself, people will set them for you.

That means you need to put a stake in the ground and OWN YOUR TRUTH.
Because if you don't make a name for yourself, somebody will make one for you.

Now, if you're the kind of person who says, "Yeah, but I'm not a leader…"

Think again.

We're all leaders. Even if the only person we ever lead is ourselves. That still counts.

The challenge is doing so authentically. After all, being yourself is hard. As Emerson famously said, "To be yourself in a world that is constantly trying to make you something else is the greatest accomplishment."

Here's a list of <u>nine practices</u> for kicking ass without selling out:

1. **Be the "You" that you always wanted to become.** Straight out of Jerry Maguire. That moment when Tom Cruise prints out hundreds of copies of his corporate manifesto called, "The Things We Think, But Do Not Say." Sure, he got fired the next day. But at least he stopped living a lie. Man. If only more people had stones like that.

   LET ME ASK YA THIS: What is still lethal inside of you that wants to be transformed?

2. **Behave in a manner that is consistent with your self-concept.** Act in harmony with the way you see yourself. Live in a way that honors your soul. You'll find it's actually a LOT easier than the alternative. See, some people fake it till they make it for so long that they never get around to making it. Just start making it. TODAY. Faking is for amateurs.

   LET ME ASK YA THIS: How could bring more of yourself to this situation?

3. **Calculate the cost of NOT standing up for your boundaries here.** Literally. Think about what, specifically, would happen to your body if you compromised your truth. Some people would feel a thud in their gut. Others a ping in their chest. Either way, your body never lies to you.

   LET ME ASK YA THIS: Are you able to hold a courageous conversation to reinforce your boundaries?

4. **Imagine what the earlier version of yourself would do in this situation.** Of course, that implies you've grown. Evolved. Matured. Ripened. And that process ONLY comes from a never-ending desire to add value to yourself. Which means you should probably stop watching television. Come on. You already know who's going to win American Idol anyway. My money's on the cute guy with spikey hair and designer jeans.

   LET ME ASK YA THIS: Do you have a remarkable devotion to personal progress?

5. **Leverage your frustration in this situation as motivation to grow into more of the person you've always wanted to be.** "Breath through it." That's what my yoga instructor always says. That every posture – difficult and pretzel-like as it may seem – can always be navigated effectively if you

just breathe through it. That's the secret: Save the drama for your mama and channel your frustration into something more productive.

LET ME ASK YA THIS: What mission were you mandated to fulfill?

6. **Make choices that add wood – not water – to your internal fire.** Life's too short to surround yourself with people who don't challenge and inspire you. Life's too valuable to work a job that robs you of your true talent and purpose. And life's too beautiful to spend watching other people pursue their passion while you sit in a cubicle waiting for your boss to go to lunch so you can go take a nap in your car.

LET ME ASK YA THIS: Does your calendar reflect your passion?

7. **Make sure the message you're currently preaching is the dominant reality of your life.** That's the difference between *orthodoxy*, which means, "correct thoughts," and *orthopraxy*, which means, "correct actions." It's about preaching what you practice, not the other way around. Because people don't give you credit for what they HEAR you SAY consistently. They only give you credit for what they SEE you DO consistently.

LET ME ASK YA THIS: What type of person do you have to become on the inside to become the person you want to become on the outside?

8. **Release the behaviors that are preventing you from making progress towards becoming the best version of yourself.** Example: Shrinking from the opportunity to share your eclectic interests with others. Example: Backing away from posting pictures of yourself being yourself. (Legal ones.)

LET ME ASK YA THIS: What are you currently doing that makes NO sense at all?

REMEMBER: Honor thy heart, not thy handbook. Surrender to thy soul, not thy script.

HELLO
MY NAME IS CHAPTER,

twelve

Are you willing to be an imperfectionist?

About once a month, I get an email from a reader who kindly points out a typo in one of my books.

This, in my opinion, is a victory. Because at least I know *somebody's* reading other than my mother.

And part of me wishes I'd thought to include those typos intentionally, just for the purpose of measuring readership. But I didn't. The typos are there (not because I'm savvy), but because I'm imperfect. Even after writing ten books. Somehow, one or two always manage to squeeze by in each one. Dang it.

But I'm cool with that. Perfection is overrated anyway.

It's also dangerous for the following <u>four reasons</u>:

1. **Perfectionism is procrastination.** Nothing by a tired excuse assembled by your ego. Just a paltry attempt to prevent productivity. And the danger is, if you don't learn to put your foot down and declare, "The hay is in the barn," you'll never, ever finish what you started.

2. **Perfectionism blocks inventiveness.** Nothing but a trap set by your neurotic compulsions. Just a feeble effort to prohibit progress. And the danger is, if you don't learn to heighten your tolerance of ambiguity, you'll never undergo creative evolution.

3. **Perfectionism stains communication.** Nothing but a brick wall erected by your narcissistic desires. Just a cheap shot at your ability to inspire people. And the danger is, if you don't start communicating less perfectly, people will stop listening to what you say.

4. **Perfectionism slaughters playfulness.** Nothing but a campaign against creativity, waged by the authoritative voices in your head. Just an incessant struggle to silence your inner kindergartner. And the danger is, if you don't learn to embrace silliness, you'll never earn the right chase greatness.

That's why perfection is so dangerous.

THEREFORE: Exerting your imperfectness is a hallmark of approachability.

In the words of U.S. Anderson, author of *The Magic in Your Mind*:

"When imperfectness enters a man's soul, he is able to show that he does not live alone in the world, but with millions of others, in whose hearts exists the same animating spirit."

What about you? Are you willing to be an Imperfectionist?

If so, consider these practices for implementing a little imperfection into your daily life:

1. **You don't have to do everything right.** My dad once gave me this advice during one of those Father/Son/Homer/Bart discussions on parenting. Pretty powerful stuff. And it made me realize something: *Flawless execution doesn't exist.* In families. In business. In ping pong. Wherever. The secret is to make mistakes, make them early and make them quickly. Then, to write those mistakes down – along with the lessons you learned from making them. And ultimately, keep moving. **REMEMBER:** Those who make mistakes don't just make money – they make history. *What have you botched, biffed or blown today?*

2. **Teach yourself to be impatient.** It's not that patience is overrated – it's that impatience is underrated. Don't wait for permission. Don't even wait for overwhelming evidence before trusting yourself. Just go. Even if what you're working on isn't perfect. Be willing to look bad on the road to immortality. Be willing to plunge forward plan-less. Or else the misguided desire for perfection will prevent you from doing, having and becoming what you and you need. *How much money are you losing by being too patient?*

3. **Become at peace with your nakedness.** An effective strategy for embodying this concept is to run through your own college campus in

broad daylight on a Tuesday morning wearing nothing but a purple thong and a headband. (At least that's what I did.) "Thy nakedness shall be uncovered, yea, thy shame shall be seen." Great scripture from the book of Isaiah. And it helps remind us that we're all going to be found out eventually. Time with either expose you or extol you. May as well beat people to the punch, right? **REMEMBER:** Telling the truth about your darkness keeps you in the light. *Which of your imperfections do you need to smoke a peace pipe with?*

4. **Make progress, not perfection.** Speaking of wearing purple thongs in uncomfortable positions. Yoga legend Bikram Choudhury constantly reminds his students, "Few of us ever do the poses perfectly. Instead, it's about how well you understand what you're trying to accomplish in each pose and how you try to accomplish your goal." As a yoga student myself, I've achieved powerful results by embracing this principle in my own practice.

"You don't just learn the ideal pose," Bikram says. "You learn what challenges you will face during the process, in addition to what clues will help you make rapid progress." So, whether you're a yoga student or not, progress revolves around asking yourself three questions: How do you gauge progress? What amount of progress is acceptable? And can you think of a way to quantify that amount so you can constantly measure it? That will focus you on moving forward without moving flawlessly. *Are you trying to keep from losing ground, or trying to make progress?*

5. **Learn to thrive in shades of gray.** Learn to walk the halls with an attitude of *confident uncertainty.* Ellen Langer explains the power of this practice in her (must-read) book, *Mindfulness*:

"You're confident that the job will get done, but without being certain of exactly the best way of doing it. This gives employees more room to be creative, alert and self-starting. Ultimately, when working for confident (but uncertain) leaders, people are likely to think, 'If he's not sure, I guess I don't have to be right 100% of the time,' and risk taking becomes less risky."

It's about increasing your tolerance for ambiguity. It's about not reaching for ready-made replies. And it's about asking questions you don't know the answer to. *Are you confidently uncertain?*

6. **Don't be at war with HOW when you should be in love with WHY.** You don't have to know *what* you're doing. You don't have to know *where* you're going. You don't have to know *how* you're going to get there. You just need to

move – and you need to know WHY you're moving. Just keep starting. The finishing will take care of itself. If there even IS a finish line. Which there isn't. *Are you stopped by not knowing how?*

7. **Be polished, not perfect.** As a professional speaker, I pride myself on performing with polish. For me, that means pausing. That means relaxing. That means preparing and rehearsing. That means listening to the audience. That means knowing my material cold. That means easing into transitions smoothly and effortlessly.

   Now, admittedly, I still make mistakes on stage. *The occasional Freudian slip. The accidental stumbling over a word. The literal stumbling over the power cord from my laptop that instantly shuts down the LCD projector ten minutes into my speech and makes me look like a complete putz.* It happens. And when it does, I acknowledge it, laugh it off and continue with the performance.

   Interestingly, after 500+ presentations worldwide, NO audience has ever been unforgiving of such imperfections. So, remember The Guitarist's Code: It's not whether or not you bust a string; it's how quickly you return to the music that matters. *Are you concerned with appearing perfect or being polished?*

8. **Forego superficiality and, just for once, try being real.** Here's the deal: Honesty makes you vulnerable. And vulnerability reinforces your humanity because human beings are, by their very nature, imperfect. Yes, it takes significantly more work to walk your truth. Especially in a world of (mostly) fiction. But, as my Aunt Vicki once told me, "If everything is perfect, somebody isn't being honest." *What social mask are you willing to retire?*

9. **Trust that people want the real you.** In *Writing for Your Life*, Deena Metzger explains that beauty appears when something is completely and absolutely and openly itself. Similarly, you need to believe that people really DO want the best, most honest, most imperfect version of you. And if they don't, you need to believe that that's fine, too. But if that's the case, now might be a good time to walk away form those people. *Which version of you do you think people want?*

10. **Allow unguarded moments.** Who knows? Maybe now is the chance to screw up royally because you've been too perfect lately. Don't worry: When you open the door to your imperfect nature and remove that which blocks the path of truth, the selfhood on which you stand will support you. And the awareness and honesty of your imperfections – ugly and terrifying as they

may be – will set you free. Well, either that, or your secretary will call the police. *What if you laid down your gloves, just for one round?*

11. Stop trying to be a leader. Instead, exert your passion fueled by your purpose. Instead, make your life a work of art. Instead, become a living brochure of your own awesomeness. If you do these things – and do them IM-perfectly – people will follow.

As Warren Bennis reminds us in *On Becoming a Leader,* "No leader sets out to be a leader. People set out to live their lives, expressing themselves fully. Then, when that expression is of value, they become leaders. The point is not to become a leader. The point is to become yourself, to use yourself completely – all your skills, gifts and energies – in order to make your vision manifest."

Wow. The un-leader approach. I like it. *In what situations do you inhibit your own authentic self-expression?*

12. Don't criticize imperfections. This increases the probability of people thinking to themselves, "Thank you for treating me like a human being." The challenge is learning to tolerate a reasonable amount of error. Otherwise people will perceive you as an unimpeachable leader with unrealistic expectations.

My suggestion is to stay away from the attitude personified by Dilbert's boss, who regularly requested, "Read my mind and then recommend the decision I've already decided on." *What would happen to your career if you were known as the biggest imperfectionist in your company?*

13. Leave room for yourself (and others) to be imperfect. Stop trying to convince everyone you encounter that you're invincible, unbreakable and infallible. Approachable means bustable. Approachable means crackable. Approachable means surrendering to your imperfections.

Instead of pulling a Lady Macbeth and screaming, "Out, damned spot!" learn to say, "Hallelujah, blessed spot!" Come on. Even The Death Star had a weakness. And that thing was freaking HUGE. **REMEMBER:** Endorsing your own weakness establishes your acceptance of the imperfect humanness of others. *Are you willing to abandon yourself to your own (and others') inadequacies?*

REMEMBER: Perfectionism is procrastination. Perfectionism blocks inventiveness. Perfectionism stains communication. And perfectionism slaughters playfulness.

Exerting your imperfect humanity, on the other hand, is a hallmark of approachable leadership.

In conclusion, when it comes to being an imperfectionist, let us remember Leonard Cohen's famous tune, *Anthem*, in which he sang:

"Ring the bells that still can ring. Forget your perfect offering.
There is a crack in everything. That's how the light gets in."

Now if you'll excuse me, I have a few manuscript typos to correct.

HELLO
MY NAME IS CHAPTER,

thirteen

How are you leveraging your vulnerability to earn people's trust?

Wearing a nametag 24-7 for the past 3,000+ days has been great practice.

Practice being vulnerable, that is.

And as I continue to reflect on the past ten years of adhesive adventures, I'm slowly starting to realize the connection between vulnerability, approachability and profitability.

HERE'S THE REALITY: Sticking yourself out there is a risk.

And vulnerability is about being open. Revealing your personhood to the world. Submitting your ideas, thoughts and passions for all to see. Surrendering your Truth – weaknesses and imperfections included – to the people around you.

Shakti Gawain beautifully defines this word in her book, *Creating True Prosperity*:

"Vulnerability means allowing yourself to be affected by the word around you."

This, of course, is terrifying for many leaders. Because you're risking your truth. You're risking being rejected. And you're risking being stared at or talked about.

Yikes.

On the other hand, vulnerability DOES lead to profitability, when practiced wisely and consistently. In fact, there's a sequence of three things that happen...

FIRST: The more often you stick yourself out there – that is, exert your distinctiveness – the more comfortable and confident you become with who you are.

THEN: When you're comfortable and confident with who you are, your truthful self-expression inspires and gives other people permission to do (and BE) the same.

EVENTUALLY: When you and the people in your life stop bullshitting each other – and start realizing that it's OK to be vulnerable – the rules change.

We begin to listen to each other from a truer place.
We start to share with each other from a stronger place.
We now communicate with each other from a more genuine place.

As a result, people will listen TO you, and customers will buy FROM you.

Sounds like profit to me.

What about you? Are you ready to reclaim your right to be vulnerable – and LEAD with it?

Cool. Let's learn how.

In his classic discourse on self-disclosure, *The Transparent Self,* Sidney Jourard hits the topic of vulnerability pretty hard. I read this book in college, only two years into my nametagging adventures. And I'll always remember it as one of the first books that taught me what it meant to be approachable.

First, we'll explore a sample of his research findings. Then I'll tell you how to translate those lessons into action items you can execute TODAY to turn vulnerability into profitability:

1. **"When a man discloses his experience to another, fully, spontaneously, and honestly, the mystery that he was decreases enormously."**

   LESSON: Being vulnerable educates others about who you are.
   QUESTION: How well do your customers know YOU?

2. **"I display my love by letting him know me."**

   LESSON: Being vulnerable is a gift that you give to others.
   QUESTION: How, specifically, are you giving the gift of YOU?

3. **"Disclosure of the truth of one's being is often penalized. When you permit yourself to be known, you expose yourself not only to a lover's balm, but also to a hater's bombs."**

> **LESSON:** Being vulnerable means being open to the fact that not everyone will like you.
> **QUESTION:** Are you willing to let go of the need to be liked by everybody?

4. **"No man can come to know himself except as a outcome of disclosing himself to another person. But, when a person has been able to disclose himself utterly, he learns how to increase his contact with his real self, and he may then be better able to direct his destiny on the basis of knowledge."**

> **LESSON:** Being vulnerable is a great way to get to know who you really are.
> **QUESTION:** What have you learned about yourself by virtue of sharing yourself?

OK! Next, here's a collection of practices for turning vulnerability into profitability:

1. **Shed your armor.** A real warrior is vulnerable. A real warrior is naked. A real warrior forgoes self-protection and plunges into the depths of dangerousness because he KNOWS that when you expect nothing, failure is impossible. He KNOWS that vigorous growth only occurs in those moments when you feel totally destroyed.

   In *The Tao De Ching,* Lao Tzu uses the metaphor of water to represent this warrior-like strength: "Water is fluid, soft, and yielding. But water will wear away rock, which is rigid and cannot yield. As a rule, whatever is fluid, soft, and yielding will overcome whatever is rigid and hard. This is another paradox: What is soft is strong."

   What are you yielding to?
   Have you reclaimed your right to be vulnerable?
   And how much longer do you want to deprive yourself of breaking out in order to protect others from who you really are?

2. **Comfort zones are highly overrated.** Wearing a nametag everyday doesn't just encourage people to say hello to me. It also invites people to stare at me, make fun of me, point at me, spatially violate me, yell at me, curse at me, share overly personal information with me, attempt to sell drugs to me, start fights with me, on one occasion, make out with me in the middle of a crowded bar, and on a few occasions, stalk me. Now, I didn't provoke any of these reactions in any way, other than that fact that I was wearing a nametag.

So, while I'm not suggesting you do the same, I WILL say that I've experienced tremendous growth in my personal and professional life by intentionally inviting uncomfortable situations.

How did you make yourself uncomfortable yesterday?
How much time do you spend in your zone of discomfort?
And how much more could you learn about yourself if you hung out there?

3. **Stop being right.** Enough arguing. Enough proving your point. Enough asserting your opinion. Enough rationalizing everything someone says into (yet another) statement you disagree with. Being perpetually right is annoying. It's unapproachable. It's antithetical to effective listening. Show me a person who always has to be right and I'll show you a person who's afraid to be vulnerable.

This used to be a spot of weakness in my own career as a professional speaker because, technically, my clients pay me to provide answers. And my audience members *expect* me to be right. Which, if you've ever attended one of my programs, is only the case about 34% of the time. So, I've learned to let it go. And I hope you can do the same in your own world.

When was the last time you were publicly wrong?
What insecurity is being disguised by your relentless need to be right?
How would you treat people if you weren't trying so hard to prove them wrong?

4. **Just sit quiet.** Your hand doesn't have to shoot up first. Next time you attend a meeting or sit on a panel, play a game called "Let See How Long I Can Go Without Contributing." This will force you to listen FIRST and hear everyone else out before stating your position. Yes, it takes self-control; but you never know – you may hear something that adds to, modifies or changes your opinion.

Are you monopolizing the listening or the talking?
How do YOU feel when engaging with a conversational narcissist?
How long are you willing to wait before contributing to the discussion?

5. **Take Bikram Yoga.** I've been practicing since 2008. It's been an enlightening journey in many ways, one of which is the constant confrontation with absolute vulnerability. For those who've never taken a class, allow me to summarize the practice: The room is 105 degrees. The class is 90 minutes. You're basically naked. You sweat constantly, but you can't wipe. You have to

stare at yourself in the mirror the whole time. And you're two feet away from a bunch of half-naked, sweaty strangers on all sides.

Oh, and did I mention that your body is contorted into positions that would make Andrew Dice Clay blush? Now THAT'S great practice being vulnerable. Find out if there's a studio close to you. It'll change your life forever. Either that, or you'll totally hate it and never come back. And that's cool too.

Do you have the courage to take a Bikram Yoga class?
What would you have to lose if you did? An extra five pounds?

6. **Grow bigger ears**. People don't listen for a number of reasons, one of which is the fear of being changed. They're afraid they might hear things they don't want to hear. Or, they're afraid that they might actually come to see something differently, and maybe (GASP!) change their mind. That's why I love wearing a nametag everyday. The people I meet – who just start talking to me out of nowhere – provide me with endless opportunities to practice listening. Even if they appear to be wackos.

Here's my suggestion: Set a weekly goal to listen – all the way through – to conversations that make you uncomfortable. Whether it's an employee sharing her non-traditional political or religious views, or a coworker expressing an opinion that you totally disagree with. Just try it. All the way through. You'll be fine. And you never know what you might learn.

Why are you listening?
What, specifically, are you doing to keep yourself open minded?
And are you aware of your personal biases that block effective listening?

7. **Be a human being.** Yes, that's actually one of my suggestions. It shouldn't have to be, but it is. After all, human beings are naturally vulnerable creatures. For example, I offer coaching and consulting services to my clients. And yet, I've never named my services as such because those two words are so saturated in the professional services market that they've lost their meaning. Instead, I humanized my position as a Thought Leader by introducing a service called Rent Scott's Brain. You can get more human than that. And clients love it. Wouldn't you rather rent somebody's brain than be told what to do?

Are you a droid?
Are you leading with your profession or your person?
And what unnecessary title is preventing people from getting to know the REAL you?

8. **Disclose your vulnerability.** "Actually, I'm terrified." Try saying some variation of that phrase more often. You'll find that the willingness to admit that you're scared, exposed and even in some cases, helpless, instantly humanizes you.

And the cool part is, when you have the courage and candor to integrate that openness into your daily conversations, two things happen: (1) you grant people permission to disclose their own vulnerabilities, and (2) they will respond to, and have more respect for you.

What terrifies you?
Who would feel more at ease if you shared that you were scared?
And what would be the worst thing that would happen if you did?

9. **Welcome, address and honor feedback.** Years ago when I worked in Guest Services at Ritz-Carlton, our GM would hold regular Listening Meetings. *No agenda. No structure. No nothing.* Anything goes. And he would just stand at the front of the auditorium in front of hundreds of employees and answer their questions. And I'm not talking about a pre-approved list of questions his assistant filtered before the meeting. Whatever people wanted.

Do you have a suggestion box or a question box?
How are you creating a Question-Friendly Environment?

10. **Acknowledge your slips.** You're not perfect. Nobody is. And the people who come off as too perfect and too disciplined and "too" anything are either annoying or lying. Even after 3,000+ days, I sometimes walk halfway down the street before realizing I forgot to stick on my nametag. Woops.

The difference between vulnerable people and everybody else is that when YOU screw up, you admit it. And your honesty not only doubles your learning, it make you more human, more relatable and more approachable. And sure, discipline is essential. But part of being disciplined is developing the ability to know when NOT to be disciplined. As legendary songwriter Tom Waits says in the movie *Coffee & Cigarettes*, "Now that I've quit, I can have one."

Do you listen to the way you speak to yourself when you make mistakes?
What would I have to learn about this mistake to make it no longer a mistake?

11. **Self-disclose weaknesses**. Incompleteness and imperfection are part of life. The secret is learning to be honest about your inadequacies. Because when you do this, it increases your credibility. That's what's great about Bikram

Yoga. You spend 90 minutes confronting yourself. Literally. Nothing but the mirror's reflection of your imperfect self: moles, scars, stretch marks and all. It's terrifying and difficult for many, but great practice with non-judgmental acceptance for all.

The cool part is, the more often you practice being honest with YOURSELF about yourself – yoga or no yoga – the more often you can do so with others. The challenge, of course, is first being courageous enough to look squarely at your own screw-ups, imperfection and vulnerabilities.

What's your system for practicing constant self-confrontation?
When was the last time you sat uninterrupted and quiet with just your thoughts?

12. **Embrace your inner beginner.** Bikram Choudhury, founder of the aforementioned yoga practice, is known for his mantra: "Never too late, never too old, never too bad to or sick to do this yoga and start from scratch again." So, whether you practice yoga or not, your challenge is to release the grip of your ego and get back to basics.

A simple suggestion for doing so is to regularly read "For Dummies" books. They're fantastic. I've probably read a few dozen volumes of that series, ranging from *Consulting for Dummies* to *Buddhism for Dummies* to *Sex For Dummies*. And what's interesting is how many people I meet who tell me they wouldn't be caught DEAD reading any of those books. Why? Because they think that makes them dumb. When in fact, the opposite is true. People who read those books aren't dummies – they're smarties.

How are you embracing your inner beginner?
How many "For Dummies" books have you read?
Are you willing to start from scratch again?

13. **Engage in unpredictable situations.** Show me a person who hates surprises and I'll show you a person who's afraid to be vulnerable. Instead, I encourage you to leave familiar territory and cherish uncertain ground. To break the veil and blaze new trails.

Once again, this is another benefit of wearing a nametag everyday. I have no idea whom I might meet or what crazy adventures may ensue. It's pretty exciting. **REMEMBER:** Certainty is boring and compliance is dangerous.

How predictable was your yesterday?
Are you allowing your fear of spontaneity to block your vulnerability?

14. Be more yielding. Accept what is. Be open to whatever emerges. Learn to trust what is happening. Don't fight where you are. Don't struggle against the moment. And stop wasting energy protesting. Stop resisting and start loving. Stop trying so hard and let things happen, as they need to.

First example: Our current economy sucks. Fine. Stop whining and start welcoming the challenge. Instead of crying, "Why me?" start wondering, "What's next?" Second example: Business sucks. Fine. Stop lamenting and start leveraging. Brainstorm a list ways to use the current crisis as an outreach opportunity.

How many futile battles are you fighting?
How are you sharpening your rut-fighting skills?
And what three actions could you execute TODAY to stir the pot?

15. Four words: I need your help. This is one of the most powerful phrases in any language. And it works because it's open, honest, admits vulnerability and appeals to another human being's inherent helpful nature. So, here's my challenge to you:

- Commit to using this phrase at least three times a day, every day, for the next three months. (It helps to do this exercise with a partner.)
- Keep a journal of every time you say it.
- Then, hold each other accountable by revisiting your entries and experiences once a week.

When three months is up, celebrate with sushi. I guarantee you will double your vulnerability, triple your humility and quadruple your income/

How many people did you ask for help today?
Do you know a universe of people you can reach out to?

16. Vulnerability isn't surrender. An important final distinction. Vulnerability is about openness. It's about the ability to let yourself be seen as you are, possibly even exposed in uncomfortable situations, and being cool with that. Over the past nine years I've struggled with this, as wearing a nametag 24-7 completely eliminates my anonymity whatsoever.

But the cool part is: The nametag paints me into a good corner. It's forces me to stay true to who I am, all the time, regardless of the situation. And what I've (finally) figured out is the following process: The more vulnerable you are, the more open you are. The more open you are, the less you have to hide. The less you have to hide, the more relaxed you become. And the more relaxed you become, the more effectively you can communicate with others. Cool.

With whom do you need to be more open?
When does the feeling of formality keep you from communicating clearly and freely?

REMEMBER: Sticking yourself out there – that is, being vulnerable – is a risk.

You're risking your truth.
You're risking standing out.
You're risking being rejected.

What's more, vulnerability requires confidence in yourself, implies security in yourself and suggests openness to others.

But let us not forget the wise words of the great writer, Henry James:

"To be opened to risk is to risk being shattered. But without that shattering there is no glory."

Contrary to popular conditioning, vulnerability IS strength. And we live a lie when we misrepresent the reality of our experience or the truth of our being.

I challenge you to open the door to your Truth. To risk feeling what you feel. To come out of the closet.

It makes you more relatable. It makes you more approachable. And ultimately, it makes you more profitable.

And you don't even need to wear a nametag everyday.

HELLO
MY NAME IS CHAPTER,

fourteen

How will you fully integrate your humanity into your position?

Nobel Prize winner Dr. Albert Schweitzer famously suggested the following:

"Search and see if there is not some place where you may invest your humanity."

Although that quotation is over forty-five years old, it couldn't be more relevant today. Especially in a business world that's getting faster, less personal and more anonymous, we owe it to ourselves, to our customers and to our employees to STOP BEING ROBOTS.

With the exception of Johnny Five, robots are chumps.

People buy *people* first. Period. And on an internal level, people QUIT people. Not compnaies.

SO, THE QUESTION IS: How are you fully integrating your humanity into your profession?

Whether you're a salesperson, entrepreneur, CEO or service provider, let's explore five practices for becoming less robotic and more authentic:

1. **Communicate less perfectly.** This isn't Toastmasters. If you use vocal fillers like "uh" and "like" and "you know," nobody is going to crucify you. *Just let it go.* Stop telling yourself that eloquence comes from flawlessness. It doesn't. Eloquence comes communicating your Truth in a way that's relatable, digestible and influential. Even President Obama says "uh" in every single interview he does.

LET ME SUGGEST THIS: Before sending every (major) email or memo, read it aloud twice. Then be honest. Ask yourself if it sounds like you. Ask yourself if it sounds like a human wrote it, or if it sounds a template from Microsoft Word wrote it.

THE RESULT: Customers will be less likely to delete your messages.

LET ME ASK YA THIS: When does the feeling of formality keep you from communicating freely and honestly?

2. **Lead with vulnerability.** As you've been learning in previous chapters, the willingness to admit that you're scared, exposed and even in some cases, helpless, instantly humanizes you. And when you have the courage and candor to integrate that openness into your daily conversations, two things happen: (1) you grant people permission to disclose their own vulnerabilities, and (2) they will respond to, and have more respect for you.

LET ME SUGGEST THIS: If business is a little slow right now (which, unless you're a foreclosure company, it probably is), own that slowness. Demonstrate your commitment to honesty, not your commitment to appearing successful. And the next time someone casually asks, "So, how's business!" respond with, "Actually, business is a little slow right now. But you know – I welcome that challenge. And the good news is, I've been putting in overtime on a few new growth strategies. And I'm confident that, with a lot of hard work, I'm going to overcome this slump."

THE RESULT: People will respect and, more importantly, REMEMBER, your integrity.

LET ME ASK YA THIS: Are someone others can be vulnerable in front of?

3. **Pepper in ordinariness.** It's true that nobody notices normal. It's true that uniqueness is what attracts people's attention. It's also true that unless you regularly exert your ordinariness, people wall have a hard time spotting your humanity. There's a balance. It's between being admirable; yet relatable. Not being utterly boring; yet not being terminally unique.

LET ME SUGGEST THIS: Remove everything from your purse, bag or wallet. Spread it out on a table in an orderly fashion. Then take a picture of it and post it on the "About Me" page of your website.

THE RESULT: Your customers will get to know the REAL you. (NOTE: If you're one of those people that always carries an ice pick in your bag, consider skipping this strategy.)

LET ME ASK YA THIS: How well do you merge ordinariness with remarkability?

4. **Publicly celebrate mistakes.** Doing so makes other people – especially your employees – more likely to open up to you with their ideas, thoughts and concerns. Why? *Because you've PROVEN to them that you support failure.* It is only when you're willing to surrender to your own humanity that people trust you more. And the cool part is, the more you practice this, the less judgmental YOU become in the future when THEY screw up.

    LET ME SUGGEST THIS: At your next sales or managers meeting, go around the room and require each person to (1) share a mistake they recently made, (2) offer three lessons they learned FROM that mistake, and (3) suggest the practical application of those lessons to the other people in the room. Then, later that week, create a hard copy of all the mistakes and lessons shared during the meeting. Staple a $20 bill to it and send it to everyone who attended. And atttach a sticky note that reads: "Thanks for being human!"

    THE RESULT: You'll make company history. And nobody will ever miss another meeting again.

    LET ME ASK YA THIS: When was the last time you rewarded someone for making a mistake?

5. **Scrap your title.** Nobody cares. Nobody even remembers it. Titles are worthless. Their sole function is to give people a reason to pigeonhole, avoid or judge you. Instead, practice leading with your person and following with your profession. That means values before vocation. Individuality before industry. Personality before position. Humanity before statistics.

    LET ME SUGGEST THIS: Whenever possible, wear hand-written nametags. They're easier to read, more human and more fun. They're also less threatening than those fancy, corporate badges. And by virtue of your unique handwriting and design, they allow you to exert your distinctiveness. Ultimately, handwritten nametags level the playing field by eliminating title hierarchy.

THE RESULT: You will prevent that bullshit, let's-see-how-many-extra-ribbons-I-can-add-on-to-my-badge-pissing-contest between competing members and employees.

LET ME ASK YA THIS: What could a nametag reveal about you?

REMEMBER: People buy people first – especially the people that act like REAL people.

Not robots. Not monuments of flawlessness.

People.

<u>SO, THAT'S YOUR ASSIGNMENT</u>: To be more human. To be more YOU.

In a rapidly changing business world where approachability is so rare that it's become remarkable, I guarantee that if you start doing this – if you start BEING this – people will notice. And people will remember.

Search and see if there is not some place where you may invest your humanity.

HELLO
MY NAME IS CHAPTER,
fifteen

How could you inspire and influence through inadequacy?

Have you ever stared at yourself in the mirror, half-naked, for ninety minutes straight?

It's painful.

Not physically. But emotionally and spiritually? MAN. It can hurt like hell.

That's why I love practicing yoga: *There's no escape.*

No leaving the room. No averting your gaze. No shutting your eyes.

Just a forced confrontation with your physical truth – scars, stretch marks, badonkadonks and all.

And I think that's part of the appeal. Yoga keeps you honest. *Vulnerable. Human.*

THE CHALLENGE IS: It's easy to execute those virtues in a nice warm room with your cushy little yoga mat and nice cold bottle of Gatorade.

But when you get out into the real world, it's not so easy.

As you've been learning, honesty, vulnerability and humanity threaten the status quo. And in our fear-based, trust-deficient and technology-governed culture, most people aren't ready to handle that kind of attitudinal shift yet.

Which is a problem, because too many people are becoming alienated from their truth.

THEREFORE: Your duty as a leader is to wake people up by (first) waking yourself up.

AND THE BEST PART IS: You don't have practice yoga to do so. Staring at yourself in a mirror, half-naked, for ninety minutes straight isn't the only doorway to authenticity.

The secret is to influence and inspire people THROUGH your imperfection and inadequacy, *not in spite OF it.*

Next, we're going to ten practices for doing so:

1. **Acknowledge and embrace all aspects of who you are.** That's the first step – to admit your truths. *The good, the bad AND the hideous.* Whether you're interacting with employees, clients, guests, attendees, colleagues, members, congregants, friends and students – even your own kids – the same universal principle applies.

   My suggestion: *The earlier, the better.* Doing so builds a foundation of credibility and trust, plus it subconsciously grants other people permission to feel comfortable in their truth too. **REMEMBER:** Living falsehoods is EXHAUSTING.

   How much extra energy would you conserve if you chose to honor your truth more often?
   Have you made the choice to take extreme care for your authentic selfhood?

2. **Probe your darkness.** If you dare, that is. If you're willing to come face to face with the ugliness that is your Truth. If you're willing to open the door to yourself and see who the hell you really are. If you're willing to make friends with all aspects of yourself. Like my yoga instructor says, "Look at yourself in the mirror non-judgmentally. As a *reflection* and nothing else."

   That's the next step in developing a working relationship with your screw-ups. It's not easy but necessary. Not fun but fundamental. And not comfortable but constructive. The good news is, when you do this, you'll live from the place where nobody can touch you.

   What shadowy parts of your life are you withholding?
   Have you made friends with all aspects of yourself?
   And do you have the courage and ability to show yourself as you truly are?

3. **Recognize your shadow.** You know that dark spot on your truth? That flawed corner of your character? Love it. Embrace it. Hell, even share it. It's a crucial component to your humanity, and if you're not willing to honor and own it, you're just another chickenshit peddler of personal falsehood.

   As Parker Palmer beautifully says, "We will become better not by trying to fill the potholes in our souls but by knowing them so well that we can avoid falling into them."

   What potholes in your life are you avoiding?
   Have you met the darkness within yourself?
   And what would be the worst thing that could happen if you opened the door to your truth?

4. **Be willing to talk about that shadow.** You know, the stuff you're terrified for people to know about you? Yep. It's time for a Skeleton Party. (I'll bring cake.) As the aforementioned Sidney Jourard explained in *Self-Disclosure,* "No man can come to know himself except as a outcome of disclosing himself to another person. Encounters help you to sharpen your sense of your own identity."

   Embrace and endorse your weaknesses. Dare to convey your essence. You'll establish your acceptance of the imperfect humanness of others. What's more, when you talk about your darkness, you increase contact with your true self, and, ironically, shed light on what (really) you need to see.

   Do you the courage and ability to show yourself as you truly are?
   When are you most true to yourself?
   And what are you afraid to know about yourself?

5. **Acknowledge your slips.** My favorite Nirvana lyric comes from the tune *Lithium,* where Cobain hauntingly sang, "I'm so ugly, but that's OK cause so are you." So, the takeaway is: You're not perfect. Nobody is. Which, in a sort of Zen way, means that everyone is perfect.

   That brings me back to another element of yoga: *It transcends body style.* No airbrushing allowed. Walk into any studio around the world an you'll immediately notice the diversity: Fat people, skinny people; big boobs, small boobs; muscular butts, saggy butts.

   And that's just the men.

Here's what I've observed: The people who come off as too perfect and too disciplined and "too" anything are either annoying or lying. What's worse, when you're perceived as TOO good, TOO perfect, TOO calculated, TOO impressive, TOO good looking, TOO whatever – people start to wonder. *They also start to question.* "Is this guy for real?""How can I compare to that?""Who's supposed to relate to this?"

REMEMBER: If people are too busy questioning you; that means they're not listening to you. On other hand, when you have the self-confidence to acknowledge your slips, you become kind of person people listen TO and are inspired BY.

What is preventing people from listening to you?
Do you listen to the way you speak to yourself when you make mistakes?

6. **Practice self-deprecating humor.** Few practices of expressing your imperfection are more effective than making fun of yourself. Personally, I do this on a daily basis. Mainly because I have oceans of material.

And what I've learned is, self-deprecating humor neutralizes conflict. It makes others want to be around you. It's a key indicator of emotional intelligence. It defuses an otherwise tense or difficult situation. It combines modesty and likeability, while at the same time demonstrating that confidence and self-assurance. Ultimately, when you own (and share) your truth, nothing in the world is viewed as a threat to your sense of self. What a relief.

How often is the joke on YOU?
How seriously do you take yourself?

7. **Reduce the distance.** Ultimately, approachability means, "to come nearer to." So, your challenge is to narrow the gap. To melt away the layers that clog, contaminate or close off the communication channels between you and … *whoever.*

Suggestion: Stop thinking OF – or presenting yourself AS – better, smarter or cooler than the people you lead. You will lose. People are inspired and influenced by those who are grounded. It is a person's faults that make her likable.

Does your life take place in the opening or the closing?
How naked are you willing to be?
And how are you leveraging your vulnerabilities to gain people's trust?

As we finish up, I'd like to share a lyric from another one of my favorite songwriters, Glen Phillips. In the song, *I Still Love You,* he sings the following:

"I've seen the dark spot on your soul. I've felt you cruel. I've held you cold. I know the parts of you that you don't think you show. But I still love you."

REMEMBER: You will influence & inspire people (not) *in spite of,* but *because of* your imperfection & inadequacy.

That's your responsibility as a leader: *To wake people up.*

And it starts by waking YOURSELF up first.

Now if you'll excuse me, I have to take my orange spandex out of the dryer and head over to the yoga studio.

... don't IN-form; they form.

Jim Henderson, a friend and mentor of mine, is the ultimate former. He founded an organization called *Off the Map*. As an author, speaker, preacher and consultant, he teaches people about "otherliness" – the spirituality of serving.

One of my favorite Jim-isms from his best-selling book *Jim and Casper Go to Church* is, "Less information, more formation. We need to major in practices and minor in principles; to major in otherliness and minor in beliefs."

Here are <u>four ways</u> you can start LIVING this attribute today:

1. **Never stop serving.** Continually ask, "How can I help you the most?" "What's the best way for me to help you right now?" and "What accountability question do you want to be asked?"

2. **Orthopraxy, not orthodoxy.** Focus your efforts on the right practices; not the right beliefs. Instead of practicing what you preach; try preaching what you practice. DO stuff first. Then tell people about what you learned form that stuff.

3. **Catch conversational deficits.** Notice when you've (1) been talking for a while, or (2) been on the receiving end for a while. Come up for air by saying, "Patty, I've been talking for a while, so I'm going to shut up now…" or "You know, you've been so generous with helping me today – what can I do for YOU?"

4. **Give others space to be who they are.** When someone shares his passion – especially when it's something unusual, obscure or completely opposite of what you do – like bird watching, for example – respond with, "Cool!" or "Wow!" These complimentary, yet objective words invite the other person to share more.

LET ME ASK YA THIS: Whom are you forming?

HELLO
MY NAME IS CHAPTER,

sixteen

What fuels the engine of your credibility?

Action is the engine of credibility.

So much so that, without it:

People will not listen to you.
People will not buy from you.
People will not open up with you.
People will not put their trust in you.

People will not take you seriously.
People will not consider your ideas.
People will not seek out your opinion.
People will not tell others to do the same.

Action is the engine of credibility.

THERFORE: It does not matter what you believe. Or intend. Or even what you say.

Believing is overrated. Intending is useless. Talking is worthless.

Doing, on the other hand, isn't.

It never has been.

Action is, has always been – and will always be – eloquence.

Your challenge is to continuously TAKE massive action. Every day. Constantly shoveling coal into your engine of credibility.

Here's how:

1. **Study the origin.** The word "credibility" comes from the Latin *creditum*, which means, "a loan, thing entrusted to another." That's interesting. *Credibility is on loan.* Which mean your stoppage in action will make the engine sputter. Which means your credibility might take years to assemble, but only seconds to annihilate. Yikes.

   How are you marring your own credibility?
   What is diminishing the perception of your expertise?
   And how might you be (accidentally) making yourself appear less trustworthy?

2. **Close the credibility gap.** A few months ago I turned my radio to NPR to listen to the daily news show, "All Things Considered." I'm not sure whom they were discussing, specifically, but the quotation was, "I couldn't listen to his testimony because there wasn't a shred of credibility in his being." Wow. Kind of makes you wonder: (1) who are they talking about? And (2) what that guy did to warrant such a gap?

   How could YOU make credibility vanish?
   What if you wrote a list on how to do so, printed it out and looked at it everyday? Think that would help close the gap?

3. **Take daily steps to strengthen your foundation of personal credibility.** In the book *Credibility*, authors Kouzes & Posner explain, "Credibility is a foundation built brick by brick. It's earned through human contact, gained in small quantities though physical presence."

   That's what leadership is. You don't have to work for some huge company. You don't need thousands of followers. One person is enough. And in that simple encounter, you listen, you transfer passion and you demonstrate emotional reliability. And over time, your foundation grows more robust. That's how credibility is earned.

   How are you using your interactions to earn trust?
   What action have you taken (specifically) in the last 24 hours to boost your credibility?
   And how many other people witnessed it?

4. **Learn to regain credibility after a failure.** Fine. You screwed up. Big deal. Happens all the time. The secret is the way you respond to it. To quote the book *Managing Up*, "The bigger or more far reaching the consequences of your idea, the more you should expect to have your personal credibility examined."

   Here's how to regain credibility: (1) Recognize it, (2) Own up to it, (3) Ask your people to help your rebuild it, (4) Make a commitment to doing so, (5) Visually remind people of your progress toward that commitment during the process, (6) Maintain consistency until they trust you again, (7) Thank them for sticking with you, (8) Never stop building credibility in everything you do, and (9) Make sure that credibility is relevant.

   How will you use action to bounce back?
   What have you done (specifically) in the last 24 hours to boost your credibility?
   And how many other people witnessed it?

5. **Create a credibility-strengthening plan.** I suggest physically writing it out, signing it and posting it in a visible location in your office. This not only allows you to clarify your plan on paper, but also serves an effective tool for keeping yourself accountable. Now, in terms of what your plan consists of, that's up to you. Just **REMEMBER:** Make it daily, make it specific and make sure it involves one-on-one interactions with people. Those encounters are the soil in which your credibility will grow.

   How are you closing the credibility gap?
   Do you need a marketing plan or a credibility plan?
   How will people know you're dedicated to your credibility?

In summary, I'd like to quote a classic song called "When You're Traveling at the Speed of Light" by the band *These United States*. In the final refrain, there's a lyric sung repeatedly for about two minutes before fading out. It goes like this:

"If the thing that drives you onward is your heart, you must not let that engine die."

Great line. And when I was listening to that album this morning, I started thinking: What would happen if I plugged that lyric into today's topic?

It might go something like this:

"If the thing that drives your credibility onward is your action, you must not let that engine die."

How are you branding your honesty?

That's the question you need to answer. Whether you're a Fortune 1000 on Wall Street, a thirty-person pizza joint in Decatur or a one-man show working out of your living room alongside your snoring pit bull, you MUST brand your honesty.

For three reasons:

People are tired of being lied to.
People are sick of wading through the ever-rising tide of corporate and political hogwash.
People are forever jaded from the countless times they've been burned, duped, fooled, conned, scammed and screwed over.

Like my friend Jeffrey Gitomer says, "If you lie to me, you LOSE me."

LESSON LEARNED: Truth is currency.

Being honest is actually easier. As Brad Blanton suggests in one of my favorite books, *Radical Honesty*, "Lying the single cause of all stress."

I couldn't agree more. In fact, every time I notice stress in my own life, I just ask myself, "What lie am I telling that's causing this stress?"

Because your body will always tell you the truth.

So, honesty is attractive for two reasons:

First, honestly is attractive because it always has been. It's a classical value. Few virtues have been around longer that honesty. In fact, there IS no Latin derivative for the word *honor*. Honesty is about as Old School as you can get.

And secondly, honesty is attractive because it is rare. And unexpected. And underrated. Which, by way of The Law of Scarcity, almost makes it remarkable. *Wow.* Isn't that wild? Something as simple and enduring as honesty has become so rare that it's become remarkable.

SO, HERE'S THE SECRET: Honesty is much more than simply "not telling a lie."

Honesty is about telling THE truth.
Honesty is about honoring YOUR truth.
Honesty is about respecting OTHER PEOPLE'S truth.

Let's explore a list of <u>nine daily practices</u> you can start executing TODAY to begin branding your honesty:

1. **Be abnormally honest.** In 1994, Progressive became the first auto insurance company to provide its rates alongside the rates of other companies. That way, consumers could easily compare and decide, even if they didn't use Progressive.

   Think that honesty has paid off?

   You better believe it. Fifteen years later, Progressive is still #1. They realize that even when you say no, you're still marketing. Even when you say no, you can still position yourself as a resource. And even when you say no, you can still strengthen your credibility.

   Do you know what you AREN'T?
   Who could you turn away today that would come back in a year?
   How much money are you losing by not being abnormally honest with your customers?

2. **Be microscopically truthful.** That's where honesty shines the brightest. In those little moments where lying would probably be easier and quicker. The secret is simple: *Character overrides impulses.* Because sometimes you have to trade honesty for being right. Sometimes you have to be willing to look like a complete and inconsistent idiot to practice what Gandhi called "living as close to truth as possible."

Don't worry, people will notice. Probably not all of them. And probably not right away. But they'll notice. And they'll remember.

Would you be willing to live with the consequences of being honest?
Will this lie require another lie?
If so, will it be worth it?

3. **Encourage truthful self-expression.** In the aforementioned *Radical Honesty*, Blanton also say, "Freedom comes from refusing to hide." Once again, I couldn't agree more. This reminds me of Avery, my twelve year-old cousin. Coolest kid ever. At his recent Bar Mitzvah, he wore a black suit, a purple shirt, a green tie and white shoes. *It was bad ASS.*

    And what's cool is, any other person in the world probably would have looked like a total putz standing on the pulpit looking like that. But Avery pulled it off. Because he knows how to exert his distinctiveness. He knows how to keep it real. And his truthful self-expression inspires other people to do the same. That's honesty.

    What is preventing you from living your truth?
    Whose permission are you waiting for?
    Why not try it out tonight?

4. **Honesty IS authenticity.** There's a word that's rapidly approaching the end of its product lifecycle. Every time I go to Borders and see (yet) another uninspired book on leadership with the word *authenticity* in the title, I want to pull it off the shelf and use the dust jacket to paper cut my pinky toe. *Vlargh.*

    That's what's cool about branding your honesty. It's not some cliché you smear all over your website. You don't have to try to be honest. You just are. You just do it. You just tell the truth. You just honor and respect yours and other people's truths. Do that, and you WILL be authentic.

    What barriers to authenticity are preventing you from being as successful as you could be?
    How could regular expressions of honesty annihilate them?
    And if they did, how much (more) money could you be making?

5. **Refine your truthfulness.** Take a minute to imagine what it would feel like to live from a place of complete, personal truth. Literally visualize how your daily life would be different. *Phone calls. Emails. Conversations. Meetings. Trips to the grocery store. Your intramural softball team.*

Think about what would happen if that kind of honesty permeated every nook and cranny of your life. Think about what would happen if that kind of honesty spilled over and trickled onto other people's lives. Then, think about what you would have to change TODAY to move one step closer to that reality.

What is preventing you from living your truth?
Why haven't you given it the finger and told it to sod off yet?
Wouldn't that feel great?

6. **Reliability implies honesty.** Brands are expectations. Shortcuts. Which means it's your job to prove customers right. To confirm their suspicions about the value you deliver and the values you stand for – namely, honesty. It also means you need to be (somewhat) predicable. In person. Via email. On the phone. Everywhere.

So, try this: In your office, post a bunch of sticky notes that read, "Is what I'm doing RIGHT NOW consistent with the honesty of our brand?" That should paint you and your coworkers into a good corner.

What is the truth at this particular moment?
How are you using that to increase your emotional reliability?
And what system could you put in place to keep yourself visually accountable?

7. **Reinforce brand moments.** Any time you do or say something consistent with your brand's honesty, tell people. For example, if you email a prospect and say, "Well, my consulting fees are available on my website," don't forget to punctuate that sentence with, "…because that's the way I do business," or "…because that's what clients have come to expect of me."

They'll appreciate your integrity. And people respond to policies. Ultimately, consistency leads to familiarity. Familiarity leads to predictability. Predictability leads to trust. And trust reinforces honesty.

How many brand moments will you experience today?
Will you be ready to express your brand's truths and values in a sufficiently beautiful way?
And when you do, what will people's reactions be?

8. **Take truth serum.** At your next Staff Training, make all your employees watch *Liar, Liar*. Then have a discussion about honesty. Start off by asking: What would happen if you were forced to go an ENTIRE workday without telling a lie? That'll promote an interesting discussion.

Then, have each person make a list of ten lies they told yesterday. From the littlest white lie like, "Well, I've gotta get back to my cubicle, Dave," to "Yes, Mr. Jackson, my manager tells me those cockroaches come free with your steak." Another fun team building exercise!.

Lastly, require each of your employees to take truth serum. Literally. Challenge them to go ONE DAY without telling a single lie. The results will be staggering.

> *How many lies did YOU tell yesterday?*
> *How many of them required a second lie?*
> *Isn't about time you started telling the truth, Abe?*

9. **Choose truth over consistency.** In the book *The Tao of Inner Peace,* Diane Draher puts it perfectly: "We must never let a cause, organization or a relationship so completely eclipse our lives that we forget who we are." Amen to that. As my mistakes have taught me, there comes a point where commitment can actually become a detriment. After all, what good is being committed if your commitment causes you to dishonor your Truth?

We need to be careful that psychological and social pressure doesn't prevent us from making mistakes. Yes, constantly remind people of your commitment ... BUT ... let go of the need to do so for sole the purpose of strengthening your own position. Embrace your imperfect humanness. Honesty is more important. Do what Gandhi did. Choose truth over consistency.

> *Are you terminally unique?*
> *Is your honesty perceived as being self-righteous?*
> *And are you really committed, or are you just trying to avoid cognitive dissonance?*

REMEMBER: People are tired of being lied to.

Try being honest instead. What a concept.

HELLO
MY NAME IS CHAPTER,

eighteen

How do you honor the spirit in those you serve?

"I bow to you."

That's the literal translation of the Sanskrit word *namaste.*

And although it's primarily used as a greeting or salutation in Indian, Buddhist and Asian cultures/faiths, there's no reason you can't embrace the spirit of *namaste* in your own daily life.

Yoga instructors are big on this. At my studio, at the end of each class – right before our instructor walks out of the room and left us to our final meditation – she will conclude by saying *namaste.* Then, as a gesture of respect and gratitude, all of the students will repeat *namaste* in unison as she exited through the back door.

Well, almost all of the students. Personally, I'm usually so exhausted, out of breath and out of fluids that I can barely keep my eyes open, much less spit out a three syllable word.

Interestingly, I've recently learned that the word *Namaste* also translates to "The sprit within me honors the spirit within you."

And I thought, "Cool. What a beautiful concept. I wonder if there are other areas of life in which we could apply *namaste?"*

That was about a year ago. Since then, I've been collecting a list of practices that transports this sacred philosophy into our daily interactions. Some are about listening, some are about leadership; ALL are approachability related.

So, as you read each of these examples, I challenge you to ask yourself three questions:

How do I feel when others do this for me?
How well am I currently practicing this in my own life?
What are some ways I could improve the way I practice this in my own life?

1. **Embrace their pace**. Listening is about helping the other person give birth to her own understanding. It's about facilitating a natural process. Enabling and nurturing the speaker's rhythm guiding him to make the best choices. Ultimately, the goal is to provide *assistance*, NOT *authority*. That way he can see, find, say, do, know, learn and discover by his own accord.

   TRY THIS: Resist the need to take over. Respect the speaker's speed of self-discovery. No pushing. No forcing. *Gentle nudging*. Embrace their pace. Suspend conversational control. Allow people to safely process their own thoughts and solutions. *Namaste. The spirit in me honors the spirit in you.*

   TRY THIS: Frame answers with alternatives. Instead of giving advice, pose questions so the other person can hear more deeply what his heart is saying. Ask, "What are your options?" This objective response doesn't take over someone's problems. It allows him to dig for the answer on his own. Also, the use of the word "options" indicates multiple possibilities for solutions. What's more, this response avoids telling someone what they, "should" do, while still offering a potential solution. *Namaste. The spirit in me honors the spirit in you.*

   How are you inviting discovery?
   How are you creating a space where people can see the solutions in themselves?
   And how would people's perception of your leadership ability change if THEY were the ones who felt like they always discovered the solution?

2. **Give people the time and space they need to fully express themselves.**
   In Parker Palmer's fantastic book about listening and leadership, *A Hidden Wholeness*, he talks about being hospitable to the soul. "Make each soul feel safe enough to show up and speak its truth," he explains. "Create a space that invites the soul to make itself known or you will scare it away and drive that which is original and wild into hiding." Wow. Imagine what would happen to your perception as a leader and listener if you practiced that.

   TRY THIS: Resist your impulse to fix. Just be. Abandon the arrogance of believing you have the answer to the person's problem. "It's not a problem to be solved but a mystery to be honored," Palmer suggests. So, don't try to save people – just be present to them. Stand with simple attentiveness. Your faith in them will bolster their own faith in themselves. *Namaste. The spirit in me honors the spirit in you.*

TRY THIS: Approachability is just as much about what you DON'T do. Examples: Don't fix. Don't invade. Don't evade. Don't advise. Don't set straight. Don't influence. Don't pressure. Don't answer. Don't save. Don't analyze. Don't insert opinions and agendas. Don't advance your self-image. I know it's a lot to keep track of, but if you fall victim to these egoic tendencies, you risk contaminating the listening space and scaring people's truth away. *Namaste. The spirit in me honors the spirit in you.*

> *Are you listening or waiting talk?*
> *Are you leading or superimposing your beliefs on others?*
> *And how do you plan to create the space people need to exert their distinctiveness?*

3. **Help people unravel deeper significance.** The only way to accomplish this is to create a safe container in which the person can share. **REMEMBER:** A person's soul is shy. You don't want to scare it away.

TRY THIS: Let what people say have an impact on you AND them. For example, when someone makes a profound comment, asks a killer question or juxtaposes words in a beautifully unexpected way, PAUSE. This silent space allows deep, creative ideas to surface. Which gives someone the stage her words deserve. Which gives that person the opportunity to let their original idea truly resonate down to THEIR core. Like my doctor says, "If you wait long enough, your patient will tell you the diagnosis." *Namaste. The spirit in me honors the spirit in you.*

TRY THIS: After holding a person in a loving space where she is compelled to listen to herself, send reinforcements for her unraveling process. Here's how: When you review your notes from the conversation, extract all of the keepers, nuggets and epiphanies that surfaced and email them to the other person. In the subject line write, "13 Keepers from Our Conversation Yesterday." Then write, "Karen, thanks for sharing your powerful insights yesterday. Really got me thinking! I wrote a few of them down for your reference…" Guarantee it will both unravel deeper significance and make her feel essential. *Namaste. The spirit in me honors the spirit in you.*

> *How are you helping people help themselves?*
> *Have you accepted silence as a normal part of your conversations?*
> *And how are you following up with people to make sure they listen to themselves?*

4. **Open your receptors to the other person's subtleties.** Listening is about listening FOR things. Even if you don't agree. Even if you don't approve. That's all part of *Namaste* – the honoring. The accepting. The loving. So, begin by listening for language patterns: Listen for what they say, listen for what they don't say, listen for what they're not telling you, listen for what the person is trying to communicate, listen for what thoughts they share first, listen for what thoughts they share last, listen for what is emphasized and listen for what is downplayed.

Also, listen for opportunities: Listen for what is pushing the person, listen for their ideas of how they want things to be, listen for how to remove resistance, listen for what the person would need, listen for others' interests and listen for areas where people are afraid and hurt.

TRY THIS: Say what you see. Use *Phrases That Payses* like, "I had an observation," "I noticed," and "My intuition is telling me that…" The three secrets is: Observe, don't accuse; insinuate, don't impose; and describe, don't prescribe. Otherwise people won't open up, become defensive and assume you're trying to "fix" them. *Namaste. The spirit in me honors the spirit in you.*

TRY THIS: Count behaviors. If you're taking notes when working with someone, keep a discreet tally of certain tendencies, i.e., "The number of times he says the word 'but'" or "The number of sentences he starts with the word 'I can't…'" After a certain point, turn your paper 180 degrees and show them your tally. Explain what it stands for and then wait for a response. This objective, non-judgmental style of feedback is not only respectful, but doesn't challenge someone's character or attitude. *Namaste. The spirit in me honors the spirit in you.*

> *What are you listening for?*
> *What are you listening with?*
> *And what do you plan to do with what you hear?*

5. **Understand, honor and respond to their unique experience of the world.** My definition of empathy is, "The ability to look at the world through different value systems." This means placing special or unique value in everything people share with you. This means not trying to change the situation, but rather, thinking new ways to experience it that would make a positive difference in how you feel.

TRY THIS: Change your relationship to your emotions. Don't allow your defensiveness to block your receptivity to someone else's truth. Especially when there's a conflict of opinions. Instead, view disagreements as if they were celebrations of ideas. You will listen with a more open (and less defensive) posture.

TRY THIS: Be on the lookout for subtle, external cues about what people are really like. Keep your receptors open for indicators of their core, their truth: What they value, what makes issues important in their lives, what their vision and purpose is, what they treasure and what makes them come alive. *Namaste. The spirit in me honors the spirit in you.*

Do your comments honor the other person's unique feelings, thoughts and emotions? Have you lost track of this conversation because of the inner conversation you're having with your ego?
And what is preventing your ears from opening in this conversation?

6. **The correct answer is whatever they learned.** Honor whatever surfaces. Dance in the moment. Believe that perfection is unfolding right before your eyes. Then, help them embrace this perfection so you both can feel rightness and appropriateness in the encounter.

    TRY THIS: Pick something ordinary that they said and brainstorm all the reasons you can of for its perfection. Then email that list to them the day after your conversation. They'll never forget it. *Namaste. The spirit in me honors the spirit in you.*

    TRY THIS: Acknowledge their rising thoughts and feelings. During a conversation with someone, presence is the secret and anticipation is the enemy. Ask yourself one question: *"What is the truth at this particular moment?"* That will help keep you present. *Namaste. The spirit in me honors the spirit in you.*

    What are you missing out on because of the need to be right?
    How are you saying yes to What Is?
    And how can you build an environment where wrong answers are impossible?

REMEMBER: You don't need to be a Yogi to honor the spirit of those you serve.

Practice a little *namaste* today.

... bring out your best.

When you're willing to stick yourself out there, you grant other people permission to do the same.

Like my buddy Jeff Skrentney of Jefferson Consulting. He projects a non-traditional image in a conservative recruiting/staffing industry. In a sea of blue and grey suits, you'll never miss Jeff with his trademark bushy grey goatee, Chicago Cubs hat and causal clothes.

And here's the best part: Those visual differentiators have NOTHING to do with his personal uniqueness. When you're around a sharp guy like Jeff – someone who's totally passionate, totally comfortable in his own skin and totally confident in his own truth – it inspires you to do (to BE) the same. THAT'S why people flock to him.

Here are three ways you can start LIVING this attribute today:

1. **Honor their awesomeness.** Every once in a while, when you meet people whom (1) you truly connect with, (2) Are really, really smart, and (3) Are the kind of people you want to get to know better, offer this simple, five word compliment: "We need to hang out." When said with sincerity, yet scarcity, it makes people feel GREAT.

2. **Grant people permission.** That's what approachability is. Permission to open up. Permission to request help. Permission to comfortably and confidently and consistently BE their true selves. Permission to share their victories and mistakes. Permission to volunteer information and voice concerns. Permission to discuss workplace problems before they snowball.

3. **Respond positively to all reports.** If you constantly say, "Don't bring me problems – bring me solutions!" you will scare people into thinking that the only time they can ever approach you is when their information is positive. As a result, you'll always be in the dark when it comes to other people's problems.

   This, of course, sucks. Your unapproachable appearance will stop communication in its tracks. What's more, you'll become the last one to find out how you're doing. So, I challenge you to consistently respond to good AND bad news in a supportive, helpful and non-emotionally reactive way. That gives people permission to come back to you with their ideas, questions, concerns and thoughts. Seek to suspend your judgment and evaluation of what people tell you until you've taken adequate time to process their information.

LET ME ASK YA THIS: Whose best do you bring out?

HELLO
MY NAME IS CHAPTER,
nineteen

How listenable are you?

"Nobody around here ever listens to me!"

If you've ever said this before, there are two possible reasons why.

First, maybe poor listeners surround you.

This is highly probable, as a large percentage of businesspeople suck at listening.

Of course, that's the easy way out – to blame everyone else. To complain, but take no personal responsibility.

ON THE OTHER HAND: Has it ever occurred to you that perhaps you're not a Listenable Person?

I'm not saying that's true. But it IS incredibly convenient to observe someone's unapproachable behavior and immediately assume that it's their fault.

When instead, you could turn inward and ask yourself: "What is it in ME that might be causing this person to be unapproachable?"

So, the secret is not to "get people to listen to you," but rather, **to identify and embody the attributes of Listenable People.**

Let's explore elements of what makes someone listenable. As you read them, ask yourself three questions:

How good am I at this?
How could I improve on this?
Who do I know that currently does this, and how do I respond to it when they do?

1. **Listen first.** Because I've written three book's worth of modules on listening, let me just give you the quickest, easiest, most effective summary of how to grow bigger ears:

   - **In ONE word**: Patience
   - **In TWO words**: Take notes.
   - **In THREE words**: Don't react; respond.
   - **In FOUR words**: Dance in the moment.
   - **In FIVE words:** Love them with your ears.
   - **In SIX words**: Will this comment disrupt or contribute?
   - **In SEVEN words**: Stop rehearsing what you're going to say.
   - **In EIGHT words**: Create a safe container where people can share.
   - **In NINE words**: Facilitate the exploration of the other person's immediate experience.
   - **In TEN words**: Enable the person to give birth to their own understanding.

   Then, when the time is right, make the transition. After someone appears to be finished speaking, try saying, "Have you said everything you need to say?" If they confirm, then ask, "Now that I've listened to your point of view, would you be willing to me share mine?"

   How big are your ears?
   How are you monopolizing the listening?
   And what would happen if you always let the other person speak first?

2. **Create a listenable environment.** When you walk into someone's office or sit down, start off by asking, "Is this a good time for you to listen to me?" If yes, proceed to speak. If not, ask them, "When would be a good time for you to listen to me?" These questions reinforce your commitment to creating listenable environments.

   Also, be sure to remove listening distractions. If you're having a conversation in your office, shut down your email and instant messenger programs. Turn off your cell. Or, if you're meeting someone in public, get there early so you can sit down first. Chose the chair that faces out into the busyness. That way your conversation partner will be facing a wall or booth backdrop where there are limited distractions. This will keep him focused on you. This will keep him listening to you.

Is this setting conducive to listening?
What around you might be distracting someone from listening to you?
How could you put yourself in the most listenable position?

3. **Get to the point.** The human attention span is about six seconds. Combine that with our A.D.D., hyperspeed, always-on culture, the answer is simple: *You need to cut to the chase quicker.* And if that means you have to take a half hour to clarify your thoughts on paper before approaching you boss, do it.

   A challenging yet fun exercise is to continuously ask yourself"Who cares?" after every point you make. Sure, it might drive you crazy, but it's good practice boiling down your suggestion, thought or argument to its essence. Because that's what people want: The Guts. The Meat. The Nuggets. The Keepers. The Lessons. Cut the crap and cut to the chase.

   What bush are you beating around?
   What elements of this message could you leave out?
   How could you send this message so it gets through the clearest and quickest?"

4. **Appeal to self-interest. HERE'S THE REALITY:** Nobody cares about you. And I don't mean that literally. I'm sure lot of people care about you. But you know what I mean. *People don't care what you've done.* They only care what you've learned, and how the practical application of those lessons can help them. *People don't care if you're having a bad day.* They only care how you're going to help them have a better day. *And people don't care about being apologized to.* They only care about answers, solutions and a commitment from you that the same problem won't be repeated again.

   The list goes on and on. In fact, I wrote a full list of all the things people don't care about in my book *The Approachable Salesperson.* Perhaps you should make your own list called,"Things People Don't Care About."Might be enlightening.

   Who are most of your conversations "all about"?
   How quickly do you invite other people to talk about their passion?
   If you had a stopwatch, how many seconds could you go in the conversation without talking about yourself?

5. **Ramp up your enjoyableness.** The word *listenable* simply means,"A pleasure to listen to." So, that's pretty simple. If you want people to listen to you, concentrate on (NOT) morphing into one of the following toxic personalities: Complainers, whiners, criticizers, know-it-alls, conversational

narcissists, assholes and emotionally overactive people. These people contribute little (if any) positive value to encounters and are either avoided or ignored.

Which one are you?
Which one do other people perceive you as?
Would YOU listen to you?

6. **Use vocal hangars.** Speaking of writing, a surefire strategy for becoming more listenable is to use Vocal Hangars. These conversational bookmarks attract people's attention by building excitement around what you're going to say next. Examples include:

- What if...
- The secret is...
- Here's the deal...
- Let me ask ya this...
- Here's the best part...
- Here's the cool part...
- Think of it this way...
- Yes, and here's why...
- Here's my suggestion...
- Here's the good news...
- And here's the difference...
- Well, there's a distinction...
- What would happen if...
- I wonder what would happen...
- Well there's a secret behind it...
- Have you ever thought about this...
- As my parole officer always says...
- The question I always ask myself is...
- Here's what I want you to think about...
- I can answer that question in TWO words...
- The question you've got to ask yourself is...
- Think carefully before you ask this question...
- I have one observation and one question – are you ready?

The secret to using Vocal Hangers is to pause ever so slightly right before you deliver the goods. This heightens the level of anticipation and energy into the conversation. What's more, the more you use them, the more you'll internalize them. The more you internalize them, the more natural they'll sound. The more natural they sound, the more they become part of your lexicon. The more they become part of your lexicon; the more people begin to expect them. And the more people begin to expect them, the more they pay attention when they hear them. Now THAT'S listenable.

How do you elicit rapt interest?
What is your trademark Vocal Hanger?
And what words or phrases used by others always captivate your attention?

7. **Establish predictable answering styles.** Answering any question creatively or counterintuitively leads to a higher level of thinking. Which elevates the conversation to a new level. Which enables both parties to discover their individual truths. Which yields more compelling results than if you would have offered a simple yes or no. Which, ultimately, makes you more listenable.

Here are several interesting, unexpected and listenable ways to answer a question. As you read them, pick and choose the attributes you like and work on creating your own Trademark Answering Style:

- "Well, there are a couple of answers to that question."
- "I think that depends on how you define the word…"
- "Well, let's take that question in pieces..."
- "You know, I'd really have to think about that."
- "Well, I think the REAL question is…"
- "I'm not sure that question matters."

Ultimately, the point of answering questions in these creative, counterintuitive and unexpected ways is NOT to dodge the truth; nor is to make yourself appear brilliant. It's about achieving a higher level of thinking for both parties. Now that's listenable!

What's your trademark answering style?
What steps could you take in the next 48 hours to elevate your interestingness?
And how many promotions are you NOT getting because managers perceive you as boring?

8. **Capture and engage attention.** From an anthropological standpoint, familiar structures lead to mental laziness. As a result, people's brains filter out unchanging backgrounds because, in their minds, there's no need to pay attention. Take CNN, for example. If you were to tune in at any point during their 24-hour broadcast and press the mute button, you'd notice that their screen cuts, changes or moves every six to ten seconds. Why? *Mental*

laziness, aka, Human Attention Span. Because CNN knows that if they don't do that, viewers will tune out or, worse yet, change the channel.

When it comes to being listenable, you have to honestly ask yourself: (1) Are people tuning ME out? (2) Why are they changing the channel? (3) What can I do to recapture and engage their attention?

What makes you predictably unpredictable?
Are you asking the same questions as everyone else in your office?
And when YOU'RE listening to someone, when is the moment YOU usually tune out?

9. **Harmonize with others.** Stop "typing." Instead, identify the individual preferences of the people you interact with and harmonize those needs with your personal style. In the bestselling *What to Say to Get What You Want,* authors Deep & Sussman explain: "If you've got a boss who doesn't listen to you, carefully consider what in your communication style might turn off your boss's ears." Good tip.

The book also suggests the following tip: "Send messages at the time, in the place, and in the format that experience has told you are best." Ha! Take that, Meyers Briggs. *What components of your personal style are making it hard for people to listen to you? What are this person's communication needs? Would it save time and frustration to just to email him?*

10. **Be more are musical.** Well, sort of. When you google the word *listenable,* the majority of the 205,000 pages that come up are related to music: Forums, message boards, concert reviews and record label blogs. Each discussion points to a variety of bands and artists that are "listenable," inasmuch as they are good for any mood/weather/situation and appeal to a wide, cross-generational audience.

In short: Listenable music is the band you watch for two hours without looking at your watch. Listenable music is the album you could spin on Repeat all afternoon and not even care that you've been listening to the same ten songs seven times in a row.

Your challenge is to extract those elements of listenability from the music world and teleport them into your daily interactions. **REMEMBER:** If having a conversation with you is like blasting Limp Bizkit at full volume, it's going to be tough for people to listen to you. *Can you relate to anybody? Would people love to be around you in a tense situation? And, during your conversations,* *are people thinking about booing you off stage, or raising their lighters for an encore?*

11. **Don't be unlistenable.** Damn it. Double negative. Sorry. Anyway, when I googled *listenable,* I also did a search for *unlistenable.* What I found were people's discussions on "unlistenable music." They were fascinating. Here are a few of my favorite reviews:

    - "If you take your date out to this concert, you ain't getting' lucky."
    - "I would never play this record for anyone for fear that they would uncontrollably start hurting me."
    - "I don't really know how the song ended, as I didn't get that far before running out of the room crying."

    Obviously, these reviews of unlistenable music are a bit extreme. But the parallels between music and interpersonal communication DO exist. So, here's my suggestion:

    STEP 1: Make a list called "Ten People Whose Conversations Make Me Want to Commit Suicide with a Stapler."

    STEP 2: Under each person's name, write three reasons WHY that person is difficult to listen to.

    STEP 3: Compile a master list called "Characteristics of Unlistenable People" and post in your office.

    STEP 4: Do the opposite. BE the opposite.

    If you do this, I guarantee that the people you work with will start listening to you more. *Who are the most unlistenable people you know? Where in your life do you make those same mistakes? What could you do instead?*

12. **Articulate strategy and ideas in plain language.** *The less jargon you use, the more engaging you become.* In the writing world, shorter sentences get read. In the speaking world, shorter sentences get HEARD. So, think like a writer. Watch those long and cumbersome sentences. Don't construct your ideas in a way that overburdens people's brains.

    For example, some leaders spew one idea after another. Meanwhile, listeners are still stuck on the FIRST one, trying to figure out what heck you meant. Be careful. Non-brilliance might be forgivable, but time wasting isn't. Keep your message lean, low-carb and plucked of nonessential words.

Are you messages meaty?
Could a fifth grader understand you?
And are people easily confused when you speak?

13. Share information in a clear and concise manner. *People are swamped, people are stressed, and they don't have time to decode your hieroglyphics.* As a writer, speaker and teacher myself, I've discovered the secret to raising receptivity. What's more, the secret to making your messages more listenable, readable, digestible and learnable.

Three words: *Meaningful Concrete Immediacy.* Here's a rapid-fire list of strategies to do so: No jargon. Chunk ideas into small clusters. No stupid metaphors, bromides or unclear analogies like Dr. Phil loves to use. No vague language. Speak with value, not vanity. Hook moments to personal meaning. Get passion involved. Give people the meat. Zero into the heart of the matter. Package truth as nuggets. *Meaningful Concrete Immediacy.* Got it? Cool.

How are you making it hard for people to listen to you?
How relevant, concise and applicable are your words?
Would you listen to you?

14. Create a zone of respect around you without being overbearing. Those who build credibility into everything they do are listened to. So, beware of unspecified attribution. Delete the following vague, non-believable phrases from your vocabulary: *Studies show. Recent research proves. Scientists say. Psychologists report. Experts believe. They say. There's an old story that says. I've heard. Most people agree. It is said that. Critics say. Statistics show. Somebody once said. The reviews say.*

Um, *no*, they DON'T. None of that is good enough. In a conversation. In a speech. In an article. In a presentation. You need to PROVE your point. With facts. Sources. Numbers. Dates. Otherwise people have no reason to believe you. **REMEMBER:** Credibility comes from specificity. If you can't cite a source, keep your mouth shut. Something isn't always better than nothing.

What is preventing people from taking you seriously?

15. When it's a technical matter, (still) speak English. *The problem isn't that people never listen to you; the problem is that you're not a listenable person.* Pamper people's short-term memory. **REMEMBER:** It can handle about seven bits of information at a time. (Ahem, phone numbers.) Your challenge is to do everything you can to accommodate its capacity.

Include a structure that will serve as an index for the material, i.e., "This process has four steps." Then, at the end, sum it up, i.e., "Ok, so, to review, the first step was…" That's the secret: Making it easy for people to organize and remember material.

How could you send this message so it gets through the clearest and quickest?

REMEMBER: The secret is not to "get people to listen to you," but rather, to identify and embody the attributes of Listenable People.

Commit to doing that, and soon you'll never have to say, "Nobody around here ever listens to me!" again.

HELLO
MY NAME IS CHAPTER,

twenty

What's preventing your ideas from getting through?

You might be the best communicator in your office.
You might be the greatest conversationalist at your company.
You might be the warmest, friendliest, most approachable leader around.

But none of that matters if your employees aren't in a state of receptivity.

You could have the fastest service in the industry.
You could have the slickest sales pitch on the streets.
You could have the funniest, most polished and engaging PowerPoint slides around.

But none of that matters if your customers aren't in a state of receptivity.

HERE'S THE REALITY: You can't make people listen to you.

You can only make an effort to raise their receptivity so your ideas have the highest probability of getting *through* AND getting *understood*.

SO, THIS BEGETS THE QUESTION: What does it look like to be in a state of high receptivity?

I asked Robert Lefton, founder of Psychological Associates. In his famous book, *Leadership Through People Skills: Dimensional Management Strategies*, he spends at least half the text exploring this topic.

"Low receptivity is the refusal to allow ideas through a mental barrier that is set up to shut them out," says Lefton. "And you have virtually no chance of communicating with someone whose receptivity is low."

"As such, you (also) have virtually no chance of doing any of the things that depend on communication: motivating, training counseling, sharing ideas, discussing, debating, considering alternatives, weighing options or soliciting ideas."

IN SHORT:: No receptivity = No nothing.

It's like talking to a brick wall. Sure, you THINK you're communicating. But in reality, you're just wasting your time. And the wall's time.

There HAS to be a willingness to work with the other person. As Lefton suggests, "Your success depends on your ability to raise the level of receptivity and make willing partners out of unwilling people."

Today we're going to explore the attributes of receptive (and unreceptive) people. And as we go through the continuum, I'm going to challenge you to plug yourself into both sides of the equation to maximize your approachability.

<u>FIRST</u>: Spot signs of low or declining receptivity.

Lefton's laundry list of low-receptivity behaviors includes:

Belligerence. Flat assertions. Impatience. Interruptions. Sarcasm. Silence. Apathy. Inattention. Nervousness. Meandering. Excessive socializing. Superficial questioning. Unquestioning agreement.

And since his book was written in 2000, I would also add to the following behaviors to the unreceptive list:

Checking email. Sending text messages. Listening to their iPod while you're trying to tell them how badly they screwed up.

ASK YOURSELF: What about this person's behavior tells me that he isn't open to what I'm trying to communicate?

<u>SECOND</u>: Spot signs of high or rising receptivity.

Next, here's a list of high-receptivity behaviors:

Qualifying their assertions or arguments. Showing that her mind is not made up by questioning her own viewpoints. Thoughtful agreement. Involvement and non-belligerent debate. Pertinent questions.

Again, since Lefton's book is a few years old, I would also add to the following behaviors to the receptive list:

Sitting up straight. Making eye contact. Holding a digital recorder, blank notebook and seven brand new pens.

ASK YOURSELF: What about this person's behavior tells me that she IS open to what I'm trying to communicate?

Ultimately, eloquence, logic – even well thought out arguments – are no substitute for receptivity.

I don't care if you're Dale Carnegie: No Receptivity = No Nothing

REMEMBER: You can't make people listen to you.

You can only make an effort to raise their receptivity so your ideas have the highest probability of getting *through* and getting *understood*. Next' we'll learn how to do so.

HELLO
MY NAME IS CHAPTER,

twenty-one

How will you raise the receptivity of those you serve?

Think of another person's receptivity as being on a continuum.

And the challenge is twofold: You need to lessen the intensity of low receptivity AND raise the mark on that continuum. Let's explore a list of strategies for doing so:

1. **Understand the influences.** In the book *Gentle Persuasion*, author Dr. Joe Aldrich shares a helpful list of factors that influence a person's receptivity. Let's take a look:

   - The existing loyalties of this person.
   - The transitions facing the individual.
   - The condition of the soil of this person's soul.
   - The nature and stability of this person's relationships.
   - The previous attempts to approach or invite this person.
   - The caricatures that distort someone's grasp of something.
   - The nature and frequency of past contacts with this person.
   - The circumstances under which someone learned something.
   - The people that person has known and their influence upon him.
   - The degree of satisfaction or lack thereof with this person's life.
   - The spot this person sits on the continuum between opposition and acceptance of something.

   So, whomever your current interpersonal situation involves – customers, employees, colleagues – I challenge you to plug those people into these factors. Even if you have to map out a few of the answers, this exercise might help clarify the true nature of their reluctance.

Then, once you've considered these factors, here's the next challenge:

First, recognize and respond to the uniqueness of each individual. Not "typing." Not "reading." *Attending to.* After all, "what you see when you see people" has a powerful affect in how you approach them. And you need to make an effort to comprehend the other person's view.

Secondly, reprogram this person's experience bank with positive examples that prove old assumptions wrong. This helps evolve his attitude toward a more favorable state. Our next few examples will explore several strategies for handling these two challenges.

REMEMBER: You've got to be willing to do the research. To uncover the true nature of someone's reluctance to be open to your ideas.

Do you understand the influences on this person's receptivity?
What would you have to know about this person to approach her effectively?
And what barriers to communicating freely and openly exist between you?

2. **Listen first.** Because approachability and receptivity are functions of reciprocity, the smartest step you can take is to actually listen, yourself. Sure, it's a risk. Sure, it requires you to become vulnerable. But that's part of the job description: Leaders go first. They ante up.

The challenge is to listen attentively, consider what is said and respond constructively and candidly. After all, approachability is much more that telling employees you have an Open Door Policy. Because as you learned: They don't care if you door is open – they care if your heart is open. And if your mind and EARS are open.

REMEMBER: Listening first increases receptivity because the other person is more likely to listen to you when he knows you're listening to him.

Are you monopolizing the listening or the talking?
When was the last time somebody complimented your listening skills?
And what would happen to your career if you became known as the best listener in your organization?

3. **Preserve people's self-esteem.** The need to feel accepted is a driving force of human action. Your goal is to let people know that their thinking matters to you. To let them know you need them. To demonstrate that they've helped or inspired you. And to offer your attention TO and acknowledgment OF their contributions to your worldview.

What's more, low receptivity is partly caused by unfulfilled personal needs. And when you're not making a concerted effort to preserve people's self-esteem, that gap will compete with you for their mind's attention. Concentration on any other topic will become difficult.

Your mission is to gratify people's esteem need by making them feel essential, making them feel heard and making them feel like they contributed and participated in the decision making process.

REMEMBER: Raising receptivity requires clearing the other person's mind so she is wiling to concentrate on the right things.

What is the self-interest in this situation?
How are you appealing to this person's highest needs?
And how receptive are YOU when people preserve YOUR self-esteem?

4. **Lower emotional reactivity.** Emotions block progress by reducing receptivity and impairing thought. In fact, the word "emotion" comes from the Latin *emotere*, which means, "to disturb."

Be sensitive to signs of readiness and receptivity. If someone is highly emotional, that's probably the WORST time to approach her with a concern, idea or assignment. Instead, wait it out. Let people breathe. Give them space to feel. Try asking, "When would be a good time to talk to you about something that's important to me?"

REMEMBER: Your goal is to encourage the full expression of emotions, dance in the moment and honor whatever surfaces.

What emotions might block their receptivity?
Are you giving people enough space to think, feel and BE?
Is this the best possible time to approach this person with this idea?

5. **Dig deep.** Without probing unnecessarily, explore the other person's mind. Draw him into the interaction. Don't contaminate your probes by underscoring them with your own agenda and ideas. Your lack of objectivity

will hinder their receptivity. Also, be careful not editorialize. Rewording what you interpreted the other person as saying might make your summary sound manipulative.

Further, as you're probing, remember to delete the word "why" from your vocabulary. Questions that begin with the word "why" are dangerous because:

- WHY = Defensiveness.
- WHY = Seen as criticism.
- WHY = Internalized as a personal attack.
- WHY = Easily countered with "because."
- WHY = Endless justifications and explanations.
- WHY = Answers that can only guess about the past.

Instead, use questions that begin with "What," "When" or "How." This uncovers information, specification and motivation; instead of producing generalizations, rationalizations, justifications. That should help you dig down deep.

REMEMBER: Probing isn't interrogating. It's about discovery and honest curiosity about getting to the truth together.

What words govern your questions?
Are you (actually) asking a question, or just veiling a threat?
And are you (actually) asking a question, or sneakily proselytizing your opinion?

REMEMBER: You can't make people listen to you.

You can only make an effort to raise their receptivity so your ideas have the highest probability of getting *through* and getting *understood*.

... point the way.

One of my other mentors, Arthur Scharff, is a master of "the point."

As the former CEO of Smith-Scharff Paper and founder of President's Council, his whole life revolves around leadership. He doesn't dispense solutions. He doesn't parade his knowledge. He doesn't interrupt with instant answers. He asks simple, powerful questions that point the way, thus enabling you to discover the answer on your own. Half Zen; Half Tao.

Here are six ways you can start LIVING this attribute today:

1. **Let them discover it.** Use Phrases That Payses like, "What do you think that means?" "What does that tell you?" and "What did you learn from that?"

2. **Give homework.** Tell people you don't want an answer right away. Let 'em chew on it for a while and have them get back to you.

3. **Ask action-oriented questions.** For example, "What's the next action?" "What are you going to do now?" and "How are you responding to this?"

4. **Ask; don't tell.** Asking leads to dialogue. Asking leads to positive framing of a conversation. Asking acknowledges someone's feelings. Asking shows that you trust others to develop their own answers. Telling, on the other hand, leads to defensive responses. Telling leads to negative framing of a conversation. Telling is judgmental and one-sided. Telling bypasses empathetic emotions.

5. **Avoid Ready-Made Replies.** Typical, corporate, canned answers like, "Well, that's our policy," or "That's just the way we do things around here," make customers and employees want to puke. Instead, consider using empathetic and objective Phrases that Payses like: "Let me consider what you said..." "That's an interesting way to think about it..." and "I can see how much this means to you."

6. **Prove that you're worth talking to.** Maximize people's ROC – Return On Conversation. That means you need to add value. And that means you need to become a contribution machine. Now, I'm not suggesting you become one of those solution-dispensing know-it-alls who always seems to know exactly what everyone "should" do in every situation. SO annoying. Instead, to prove to people that you're worth talking to, make it your goal to achieve ONE moment of stunned silence in every conversation. Perhaps through your penetrating questions. Or your unexpected, contrarian insights. Maybe you're partial to sharing thought-provoking one-liners or proverbs that start people's hamster wheels rolling for the rest of the day. Whatever practice best fits your passion, personality and preferences – OWN it. Become known for it. People will look forward to every conversation they have with you.

LET ME ASK YA THIS: Are you someone who gives answers or offers pointers?

HELLO
MY NAME IS CHAPTER,

twenty-two

How does your playfulness product profit?

I like to bite my dog.

She asks for it. And I figure, if she's always (playfully) biting me, there's no reason I can't return the favor. I usually go for the ankles.
It drives Paisley crazy.

Now, you're probably wondering why the heck I'm telling you this.

SIMPLE: I always start with silly.

In emails. In writings. In speeches. In conversations. In phone calls. In conference calls. In sales pitches. In meetings. In customer encounters. In coaching sessions.

I start with silly.

What about you? How early are you expressing YOUR playfulness?

How early are YOU being silly, funny and childlike?

ANSWER: Not early enough.

In my experience as a Professional Dork/Nerd/Geek/Putz/Goofball/Whatever, when you start with silly, <u>six things</u> happen:

- **You diffuse defensiveness.** Letting go of having a purpose = Letting your guard down. Instant comfort. Instant relaxation. Instant vulnerability. =

- **You return to your core.** Childlikeness takes you back to a purer, more authentic, more creative and less judgmental place.

- **You relax the situation.** Humor, silliness and lightness relax people; and relaxed people think and learn better.

- **You break down barriers.** If someone is laughing with you, that person is also agreeing with you. This reduces psychological distance between parties, thus increasing approachability for all.

- **You soften the ground.** Relieve tension early and you will set a foundation of comfort that lasts for the entire email/conversation/call/article/speech.

- **You stimulate memory.** Famed cartoonist Alfred Mercier once said, "What people learn with pleasure they never forget."

OK! Ready to become seriously playful? The following <u>five practices</u> will help you start with silly:

1. **Begin small.** Do something unnecessary and superfluous. Sure, it may start out little, but it also may become big. For example, if someone asks you, "So, what do YOU do?" before you give your REAL answer – just for the sake of starting with silly – try responding with one of these answers first:

   - "I do windows!"
   - "As little as possible…"
   - "I do whatever my wife tells me to do…"

   It's unlikely you'll get a standing ovation, but the other person will (at the LEAST) smile, chuckle, or, better yet, start playing along with you. Great way to kick of a conversation with someone you've just met. *How playful are your answers to mundane questions?*

2. **Leverage brand moments.** Next time the secretary or gatekeeper says, "May I ask who's calling?" use this as an opportunity to start with silly. Insert your *That Guy*. For example, I always say, "Yeah, tell Mr. Jackson it's The Nametag Guy." Nine times out of ten, when the other person picks up the phone, they're already laughing. You challenge is to leverage similar brand moments. For example:
   - The subject line of your emails.
   - The "FROM" line on your email account.
   - The "FROM" message on your cell phone, i.e., "First message ... received ... at ... ten ... thirty ... AM ... from ... *The Golf Guru!*"

3. **Get over your boringness.** Don't throw me that, "But I'm not funny," lie. Everybody is funny. Everyone has funny stories. Everyone possesses inherent hilarity. The challenge is learning how to discover and then deliver it. That doesn't mean tell jokes. That doesn't mean, "Use humor." That means BE funny. It's not something you DO; it's something you ARE. Regularly as yourself questions like these:

   - What's funny about what just happened?
   - Who would think this is absolutely hilarious?
   - What other funny example is exactly like this?

4. **Be funny early.** Take a lesson from comedians, writers and professional speakers. They're funny within the first seven seconds of opening their mouths. If they're not, they're no good. Now, that doesn't mean evoking sidesplitting humor right away. But it DOES mean a playfulness, excitement and lightness that INFECTS the audience right away. After all, humor is the only universal language. So, consider these examples:

   - Re-read the introduction of this article. It's not exactly Humor Hall of Fame Material, but it's fun. It's playful. It's light. That's how you start a piece of writing.
   - Go on YouTube and watch ANY video of George Carlin doing standup. He has the audience laughing within seven seconds every time. Classic.
   - Google "Dave Barry Article." The first sentence in every column he's every written is hilarious. Typical Dave.

REMEMBER: Starting with silly has a cumulative effect.

When people become silly, they become less defensive.
When people become less defensive, they become more relaxed.
When people become more relaxed, they become more engaged.
When people become more engaged, they become more likely to listen to you.
When people become more likely to listen to you, anything is possible.

NOTE: This practice of silliness doesn't mean being a big goofball all the time.

Just some of the time. (Insert Sarah Palin wink here.)

ALSO NOTE: Starting with silly (can) backfire.

Your job is to discern the situations in which silliness is or isn't appropriate.

And sometimes, if you start with silly - and truly feel that it WAS appropriate at the time - and someone simply DOESN'T get it (or looks at you like you're nuts), let it go. Maybe it was you, maybe it was them. Move on.

Ultimately, whether you're giving a speech, writing an article, making a sales call or leading a teleconference, the sooner you "lay tile" of comfort and playfulness, the smoother the message will be digested.

Maybe Mary Poppins was right. Maybe a spoonful of sugar really DOES help the medicine go down.

So, wouldn't it make sense to give people that spoonful as soon as possible? I challenge you to start with silly. Learn it, practice it, BE it, today.

Now if you'll excuse me, I have a dog to go bite.

How many relationships are you missing out on because you don't know people's names?

Names are everything.

Your name is your truth.
Your name is your identity.
Your name is the very first (and, ideally) the ONLY label that you, as a human being, should be known for.

For that reason, after nine years of wearing a nametag, here's what I've discovered:

When people know each other's names, the rules change.

Wow, Scott, is ALL your material this deep?

I know. Super obvious, right?

Exactly. And if it's obvious to YOU, that also means it's obvious to your customers.

Look. You know names are important.

MY QUESTION IS: Are you practicing that?

Think about it. I guarantee you have somebody in your life right now - a coworker, a customer, some guy that you see at the gym every morning – whom you've "known," maybe even for a few years, but you don't really KNOW – because you have no clue what his name is.

And the problem is, every time you engage with that person, that fact is always in the back of your mind. Bugging you. Driving you crazy. And it prevents you from TRULY connecting.

Here's a perfect example: Remember the episode of Seinfeld where Jerry was dating a woman whose name he couldn't remember? All he knew was that it rhymed with a female body part. He was going crazy!

First, he began brainstorming with George, trying to come up with it.

Mulva? Celeste? Gipple?

Next, when Jerry was with this nameless woman, his internal monologue never shut up. He began sneaking through her purse, even asking leading questions, trying to get to the bottom of this interpersonal mystery.

Finally, at the end of the episode, it hits him. He opens his window and screams out into the streets of Manhattan, "DELORES!!"

SO, MY QUESTION IS: What's causing conversational tension in your relationships?

Or, to take it one step further: What's preventing your relationships from getting started?

Sometimes, not knowing a name prevents you from even approaching a person in the first place. This is due to a simple sociological equation:

NO CONFLICT = NO AVOIDANCE.

Yep. More Rocket Surgery.

But this interpersonal truism, simple as it sounds, becomes even more powerful when you reverse it:

MO' CONFLICT = MO' AVOIDANCE.

Who are YOU avoiding? Who's avoiding you? And how many relationships with potentially cool people are you missing out on because of that?

Therefore: Names hold the key. Names are the baseline. Names are everything. Names reduce psychological distance between people.

Without a name, you can only get to know someone SO well.
Without a name, there's a relational threshold level you'll never surpass.
Without a name, your relationships will continue to feel awkward and inauthentic.

But.

When people know each other's names, the rules change. Once you get it, make the choice to commit it to memory, and of course, USE that name in conversation, a few cool things start to happen: You expedite and deepen the connection. You diffuse defensiveness. And you honor the Truth of each other in that experience.

Interested in making connections and building relationships like that?

Cool. Here's what to do:

1. **ADJUST your attitude.** Stop convincing yourself that you're "horrible with names." This negative attitude will only become a self-fulfilling prophecy that holds you back.

2. **ASK for names earlier.** The longer you wait, the more awkward it gets. Make sure you look the person in the eye for at least three seconds when they say their name. This helps your visual memory store the information accurately.

3. **ARTICULATE names often, but not TOO often.** Over usage makes people question your intentions. Depending on the length of the conversation, a few times is enough. Don't overdo it like a rookie insurance salesman who just got out of training and spends his days slinging bunk policies at Chamber meetings.

4. **ADMIT your name-related brain farts when they happen.** Tell the truth, tell it all and tell it now. Take the blame. It happens to everybody. And make sure to use language like "Will you remind me your name please?" instead of, "What's your name again?" This keeps the blame on YOU and doesn't make the other person feel as if they were instantly forgettable.

5. **ADVANCE your memory skills.** How many books have you read about remembering people's names? One a year should do the trick. I suggest Ben Levy's book.

REMEMBER: A person's name is his identity and his truth.

Take it from a guy whose name NOBODY seems to forget.

LET ME ASK YA THIS: How many relationships are you missing out on because you don't know people's names?

HELLO
MY NAME IS CHAPTER,

twenty-four

How beautifully
do you treat people?

1. **Be trusted to represent people's interests, even when they're not around.** *This will encourage people to confide in you, even when YOU'RE not around.*

   PRACTICE: Don't act embarrassed. If someone asks you a question about a potentially uncomfortable topic, don't try to diffuse the discomfort by making a joke out of it. That tactic only works in reverse and makes the conversation more uncomfortable. Instead, work on your poker face. Honor their question despite the fact that you might be totally confused or giggling like a little schoolgirl on the inside. This form of openness will show The Asker that it's both acceptable and comfortable to discuss difficult issues.

   LET ME ASK YA THIS: Who trusts you?

2. **Preserve people's self-esteem.** *The need to feel accepted is the driving force of their actions.*

   PRACTICE: Let them know you need them. Let them know they've helped or inspired you. Offer your attention TO and acknowledgment OF their contributions to your worldview. Each of these practices can be accomplished in two words: "Take notes." Taking notes is proof. Taking notes keeps you mindful in the conversation. Taking notes honors someone's thoughts. Taking notes is respectful. Taking notes increases someone's self-esteem. Especially when you email them a copy of your notes five minutes after the conversation. Wow.

   LET ME ASK YA THIS: How are you helping people fall in love with themselves?

3. **Tolerate honest mistakes as learning experiences.** *People don't need to be reminded how badly they screwed up.*

PRACTICE: Instead, people need to be reassured that you're going to love them when they DO screw up, help them prevent the same mistake from being made again, and partner with them to brainstorm lessons learned from those mistakes. Try this. At your next meeting, go around the room and require each person to (1) share a mistake they recently made, (2) offer three lessons they learned FROM that mistake, and (3) suggest the practical application of those lessons to the other people in the room. Then, later that week, create a hard copy of all the mistakes and lessons shared during the meeting. Staple a $20 bill to it and send it to everyone who attended. And what you do is, attach a sticky note that says, "Thanks for being human!"

LET ME ASK YA THIS: How are encouraging and rewarding mistakes?

4. **Treat people with respect and fairness, regardless of their position or influence.** *Titles are worthless labels whose sole function is to give people a reason to pigeonhole, avoid or judge you.*

PRACTICE: Acknowledge everybody. This one shouldn't even be on my list. But, because not everybody practices this simple act of approachability, I've included it. So: Slow down. Stay present. Hold your eye contact with everyone you encounter for one additional second. ONE second. That's what Bill Clinton does. Also, see if you can acknowledge every single person you encounter for one whole day. It's harder than you think. Then again, it all depends on what you see when you see people. **REMEMBER:** Unspoken hierarchies hamper the freedom of expression and, as a result, create a distance between people.

LET ME ASK YA THIS: What unnecessary title is preventing people from getting to know the REAL you?

HELLO
MY NAME IS CHAPTER,

twenty-five

How are you making people feel essential?

Yes, making someone feel "important" and "valued" and "needed" is a HUGE part of being an approachable leader. But that's not enough.

If you truly want to win with people, you need to make them feel *essential*.

Here's a list of ten practices to do so:

1. ***Three simple words.*** "I appreciate you." Not, "I appreciate that..." and not "I appreciate what you've..." No. "I appreciate YOU." Small change, huge difference. My friend John always closes his emails with this phrase and it makes me feel like a million bucks, every time. *Who do you appreciate?*

2. ***Four simple words.*** "I believe in you." NOTE: This doesn't work unless you look people straight in the eye. My friend Harlan says this to his students all the time, and they LOVE him because he believes in them. *Who do you believe in?*

3. ***Take notes.*** Taking notes is proof. Taking notes keeps you mindful in the conversation. Taking notes honors someone's thoughts. Taking notes is respectful. Taking notes increases someone's self-esteem. Not to mention, if you don't write it down, it never happened. *Do you carry a notebook or jotter with you at all times?*

4. ***Come back to notes.*** At a later date, refer back to the notes you took while listening to somebody. If possible, physically show that person the notes you took. Explain how you've applied their ideas since originally writing them down. *How are you reinforcing the size of your ears?*

5. **Tell people to write things down.** This practice takes note taking one step further. Next time someone says something powerful, instead of YOU jotting it down, tell HER to jot it down. It not only honors her thoughts; it gives her a chance to capture something valuable that she may not have recognized until you said something. *How are you encouraging people's inner poet?*

6. **Ask people to repeat things.** Not because you didn't understand their point; but because their insight was powerful. This demonstrates your desire for clarity. It also gives them a chance to rephrase, repeat or retweak their original idea, making it as strong as possible. *How do you ask for clarification?*

7. **Cheer people on.** The more cheerleaders people have, the easier it is for them to win. For example: Ever seen The Packers play a home game at Lambeau Field in December? Insane. Even if the opposing team wins, you KNOW their players were scared shitless the whole time. *Are you that supportive of YOUR people?*

8. **Bring people joy.** If you concentrate on doing this at least three times a day, your life won't just BE swell; it will swell with happiness and purpose. And so will the lives of the people you touch. Try playing the "Let's See How Many People I Can Make Smile Today" game. *How many people did you look in the eye and say thank you to yesterday?*

9. **Acknowledge everybody.** This one shouldn't even be on my list. But, because not everybody practices this simple act of approachability, I've included it. So, slow down. Stay present. Hold your eye contact with everyone you encounter for one additional second. ONE second. That's what Bill Clinton does. And see if you can acknowledge every single person you encounter for one day. It's harder than you think. Then again, it all depends on what you see when you see people. *How many coworkers did you go out of your way to avoid yesterday?*

Essential.

It's a word that derives from the Latin *essentia*, which means, "essence."

Yes.

That's what being an approachable leader is all about.

Honoring and loving and acknowledge the essence of another person.

... make you like YOU.

If you want to make an unforgettable first impression, forget about whether or not the other person walks away liking YOU. The secret is whether or not the person walks away liking THEMSELVES. My Aunt, Vicki Diedrich, does this without even trying. She's a professional artist, whose work is displayed at *Limited Additions Gallery*. And she not only has the ability to find something remarkable and beautiful in everyone she meets; she also has the grace to compliment people on that particular thing with the utmost warmth and sincerity. Sigh.

Here are three ways you can start LIVING this attribute today:

1. **Make sure people like themselves when they are with you.** It's not how you feel about you; it's not how they feel about you; it's about how THEY feel about THEM. That's all that matters. A truly approachable leader is one with whom another never feels small. One who forces people to have a good opinion of themselves.

   Suggestion: Don't just take notes on what people say; tell THEM to take notes on what THEY just said. Here's how you do it: After somebody shares a powerful insight, look at them and say, "That's great. Have you written about that yet?" or "WRITE THAT DOWN!!!" Odds are, they'll smile, possibly blush, and learn to honor their brilliance more often.

   I practice this with my colleagues at least three times a week, and it never fails to energize people's postures – both physically and spiritually. That's the best part. Their shift in body language as they begin writing demonstrates not only gratitude, but also personal pride. Remember: It's about how THEY feel about THEM. *How do most people feel when they're around you? How do you leave people? And what, specifically, are you doing every day to make others feel essential?*

2. **Help people like themselves when they're with you.** Because that's all that really matters. Not that they like YOU; but that they like THEM. People feel more comfortable around those make them feel good about themselves. Here's how:

   - *Compliments, not flattery.* Flattery is manipulation. Praise people specifically and authentically or don't say anything at all.

   - *Creat conversational deficits.* Play games like, "Let's See How Long I Can Go Without Talking about Myself," and "Let's See How Quickly I Can Get This Person to Talk About Her Passion."

Scott

- **Honor their thoughts.** Let's say someone suggests a resource/idea, makes a great joke or shares an inspirational thought. Do this: (1) immediately take out your jotter, (2) ask them to repeat what they said slowly, (3) write it down, right in front of them. You'll make their day.

- **Affirm people earlier.** Lay a foundation of affirmation. In conversations. In sales calls. In meetings. In relationships. Ensure that people feel important, valued and validated. Use *Phrases That Payses* like, "You're raising an important issue," "Great question!" "I'm really glad you brought that up," "I'm SO glad you asked that question," and "I was hoping you'd ask me that!"

3. **Judge nothing; accept everything.** When you label, you judge. When you judge, you react. When you react, you're unconscious. And being unconscious is unhealthy. Here's how:

   - **Begin without judgment.** That means using judgment-free, label-free language. In the words of Eckhart Tolle, "When you look at it or hold it and let it be without imposing a label on it, its essence silently communicates itself to you and reflects your own essence back to you."

   - **Listen to who you are before responding.** An audience member of mine suggested this during a recent workshop. Blew the entire group away. What a concept! Can you imagine how honest, how authentic and how approachable people would be if they remembered to do this in their conversations? Man. Listen to who you are before responding. It bears repeating. *Are you listening to yourself first?*

   - **Understand people better.** It starts with maintaining an attitude of curiosity. That means exploration, not accusation; fascination, not frustration. Becoming insanely interested in why people do and say what they do and say. Then, it continues with patient listening. That means questioning. That means pausing. That means listening (and hearing) people's language patterns and conversational tendencies. Finally, it means clarifying. Asking people if what you've interpreted is what they meant to communicate. *Why are you listening?*

   - **Ignore people's titles.** President? CFO? Receptionist? Janitor? Who the hell cares! The only label people should ever be called by is their name. Because they're a human being. That's it. Titles alienate people. Titles are overrated. Next time someone asks you something like, "So then, are you a Buddhist?" reply with, "Nope, I'm a human!" *What unnecessary title is preventing people from getting to know the REAL you?*

LET ME ASK YA THIS: Do people like themselves when they are with you?

HELLO
MY NAME IS CHAPTER,
twenty-six

Are you listening or anticipating?

Sometimes the most valuable lessons come from the most unexpected sources. Like from my yoga instructor, Rebecca. She (unintentionally) taught me a great lesson about listening.

During a recent class, she noticed that a few students (me included) were coming out of our postures a bit early. And by "a bit," I mean about half a second. Which, in a 104-degree yoga studio after 87 minutes of hard, sweaty work, feels like an eternity!

However insignificant that chunk of time seemed to us, Rebecca's comment to the class was: "Don't anticipate my words. Stay in the now. Stop thinking about what movement is coming next. Wait until I say 'change' to come out of your posture.

Quitting early—even a half a second—sacrifices your integrity and shows disrespect to your fellow yogis."

That's why I love yoga so much: When class is over, you can "take your practice with you." Out of the studio and into the world.

Especially with Rebecca's suggestion of nonanticipation. This is a surefire practice to help you grow bigger ears. One of the major blocks to effective listening is anticipating.

Anticipating what you're going to say next. Anticipating what the other person is going to say. Anticipating what the other person is trying to say. Anticipating how you're going to inject your opinion. Anticipating how you're going to prove the other person wrong. Anticipating how you're going to relate to what the other person is saying.

Anticipating how you're going steer the conversation in the direction of your personal agenda.

Man. Kind of hard to listen when all of that is going on inside your mind, isn't it? That's why anticipating is a dangerous barrier to growing bigger ears. To go a bit further, let's explore the three definitions of the word "anticipate":

- "To imagine or consider something before it happens and make any necessary preparations or changes." Wow. Sounds like a lot of work! Sounds like your mind is too busy to actually listen.

- "To think or be fairly sure that a certain thing will happen or come." Hmm. Sounds like you're prejudging the person, the conversation and the environment as opposed to organically allowing the discussion to evolve on its own.

- "To make use of something before it has actually been received." Yep. Sounds like rushing to me. Sounds like assuming. Sounds like your mind is searching for something else to do.

OK. You get the point: Anticipating blocks listening. So here's a list of eight practices to help you listen more and anticipate less:

1. **Pump up your patience.** Listening takes self-control and discipline. That's why you must "plaster yourself with patience," as Ralph Waldo Emerson suggested. Anticipating is a reflexive reaction, so you need to train yourself to become more patient in your conversations.

2. **Get used to silence.** Saying no to anticipating means saying yes to silence. Now, for many people, this is a difficult thing. If you can learn to practice silence in your daily life, reflection and presence will grow stronger and ultimately attract deeper listening in your interpersonal life.

3. **Think less future, more now.** Anticipating is focusing on the future, which makes it impossible to focus on the now.

4. **Reverse it.** Ultimately, the big challenge of anticipating is shifting the focus from you to the other person—practicing "otherliness" in your beliefs, words, actions and being. So instead of trying to guess what the speaker will say next, maintain presence by helping the other person reclaim the present moment. This will simultaneously keep you focused on the now.

5. **Beware of overcommunicating.** Ever heard the adage "You can't overcommunicate"? Total lie. You can absolutely overcommunicate! And anticipating is a common way to do so. Because you're in a rush. Trying to "hurry" listening. Trying to read people's minds. Big mistake! So beware of the following overcommunicative actions that stem from anticipation: Trying to be too clever. Asking too many questions. Being quick to prove someone wrong.

6. **Watch your (body) language.** Beware of unconsciously personifying your anticipation and impatience before the person has finished speaking. Doing so immediately sends the message to your conversation partner that you've just tuned him or her out. Avoid the early usage of gestures such as: Crossing your arms. Averting eye contact. Shifting in your chair.

7. **Watch your (verbal) language.** Similarly, certain words and phrases—even if you were listening attentively—stunt the growth of your bigger ears. They send the message to your conversation partner that you were doing more anticipating than listening. Avoid too-quick reassurances such as, "Yeah, I knew that was coming."

8. **Conduct ongoing assessments.** Finally, an effective measure for keeping your anticipation in check is to honestly ask yourself how well you really listened during the conversation. I suggest keeping a list handy with questions such as these: Are you listening or trying to fix? Are you listening or waiting to talk? Are you listening or controlling the conversation?

Listening is about attention. Look; don't think. Watch; don't analyze. Discovery; not answers. Curiosity; not judgment. Observe; don't interpret. So surrender to the moment. Surrender to the now. Presence. Awareness. Stillness. Patience. Nonjudgment. Stop anticipating and start listening. Now if you'll excuse me, I have a yoga class to get to.

HELLO
MY NAME IS CHAPTER,
twenty-seven

How do you assist others in giving birth to their own understanding?

Whether you're a manager, coach, leader, mentor (or just someone who LISTENS a lot), here's your simple goal:

Enable people to give birth to their own understanding.

I call this process "Midwiving" because, if you think about it, communication isn't really *that* different from having babies.

There's just less screaming, fewer epidurals and not as much bodily fluid.

(Hopefully.)

ANYWAY. Regardless of your role, when you're listening, you're there as a facilitator. A guide. An enabler. Not actually giving birth yourself, but helping someone else do the work on their own.

I've experienced this first-hand in my Business Coaching practice. When I sit down to work one-on-one with other entrepreneurs and writers – in person, on the phone or via Skype – I always make it a point to review the following philosophy before starting our session:

Midwiving enhances people's solution-finding abilities. If you've modeled the right behaviors, asked the right questions and given people the appropriate tools, they will become self-sufficient in the future. Eventually, they learn to trust their own resources. *Are you giving people fish or TEACHING them to fish?*

Midwiving boosts people's self-esteem and self-confidence. Because THEY did it. It was THEIR idea. THEIR epiphany. And this small victory (one of many) contributes to their overall self-worth. *How are you putting people in positions where they can win?*

Midwiving increases the likelihood that people will follow through with solutions. People support, participate IN and take ownership OF what they create. And the best part is, once someone has invested herself, her emotions and her passions into the equation, solving for "x" doesn't just become easy, it becomes a priority. *Are you transferring ownership TO others, or is your conversational narcissism competing WITH others?*

Midwiving appeals to people's natural cognitive patterns. Nobody likes be TOLD what they SHOULD do – but rather, ASKED what they COULD do. And the problem is, when you tell someone what something is, that's where her thinking stops. That's where her creative ideas die. Hence: Midwiving. Instead of preaching reality, you're practicing possibility. Instead of firing commands; you're presenting choices. *Are you using Asking Language or Telling Language?*

Midwiving assures people's beliefs. People believe more of what THEY say than what YOU say. As such, your challenge is to convince them (or, to help them convince themselves) using their words. They can't really argue with that! *How are you influencing people?*

Midwiving seeks people's self-exploration, THEN problem solving. The tendency to want to solve everybody's problems in the first thirty seconds of a conversation is dangerous. As a coach, I admit being guilty of this! But the problem is, it's so natural. And this instant gratification trend is partly a function of our hyperspeed culture; and partly a function of our ego's desire to fix, solve and maintain control. So, be careful. Wait it out. The solution WILL come - hopefully, not from you. *Are you solving problems prematurely?*

OK! Now that you have an understanding of the Midwiving Philosophy, let's explore three practices for enabling your customers, coworkers and employees to give birth to their own understanding (without the need for anesthesia, towels and scrubs!)

1. **LAY ... a foundation.** This is about making people feel comfortable. Powerful. Engaged. Creating a space, a climate, an environment that:
   a) Enables dialogue.
   b) Encourages creativity.
   c) Fosters openness and safety.
   d) Builds approachability through granting permission.

TRY THESE PHRASES THAT PAYSES:
"What questions do you have that I've not answered yet?"
"Sounds like you've got some ideas about this.
"Wow. I had no idea – thanks for telling me."
"You know, I'm really glad you spoke up."

2. **LET ... people explore.** Step back. Allow them to analyze their idea and watch as they mobilize their inner resources. It's a beautiful thing! You:
   a) Attend to their reality in the moment.
   b) Explore the other person's experience.
   c) Eliminate the possibility of getting defensive.
   d) Enable them to see the pluses and minuses on their own.

   TRY THESE PHRASES THAT PAYSES:
   "Can explain your thought process on that idea?"
   "I'm curious what you're thinking…"
   "I noticed…""Tell me about…" and "I wonder if…"
   "What are your options?"

3. **LEAD ... them to solutions.** Once you've allowed someone to hear himself, the answers WILL surface. And most likely, the solutions lay within the whole time, it just took some:
   a) Attending to your OWN internal experiences.
   b) Patience through pausing, breathing and waiting.
   c) Excavation through asking penetrating, challenging questions.
   d) Dancing in the moment while judging nothing and accepting everything.

   TRY THESE PHRASES THAT PAYSES:
   "When you said (x), that triggered the following thought for me…"
   "Mmm, tough problem…"
   "So, what are you going to do about it?"
   "Yes, that is a problem. So, how are you going to resolve it?"

REMEMBER: If you're listening, people will tell you their problem. But if you're monopolizing the listening, people will GIVE you their solution.

So, consider yourself a Midwife. Help others give birth to their own understanding. And ultimately, the reward won't just be a little bundle of joy…

It will be a little bundle of truth.

How are you helping people lead themselves?

If you want to grow bigger ears, remember these four words:

Let THEM say it.

Even if you have the answer. Even if you're totally right. Even if what needs to be said is SO obvious. Let them say it. Think of yourself as a "Listening Midwife." Your job is to *assist people in giving birth to their own understanding.*

As The Listener, you're trying to uncover truth together. So, the challenge is to give people a chance to peel back another layer of intentions, desires and feelings. The challenge is to lead them down the road to understanding. The challenge is to stay neutral so your objectivity enables people to discover their own solutions and, ultimately, lead themselves.

AND HERE'S THE BEST PART: When you "let them say it," a few cool things happen...

First:
Their answer is more rich.
Their answer is more right.
Their answer is more precise.
Their answer is more accurate.
Their answer is more expeditious.
Their answer is more THEIRS.

Second:
You help them access their own ideas.
You help them end up with better ideas.
You help their mind to think for the second time.
You help them set up conditions to find the answer with the same brain that asked the question.

Ultimately, by not taking sides, by "letting them say it," you bolster their self-reliance.

Here's a list of *Phrases That Payses* to enhance your listening practice:

- What else do you think about this?
- So, what does that tell you?
- So, what do you think that means?
- Is there anything else?
- What are you going to do?
- What do you think is the best solution?
- What would you do if YOU were you?

REMEMBER: If you want people's dreams, desires and truths to come to the surface – as well as stick around ON the surface – you've got to enable them to think for themselves.

You're a midwife, remember? Assist them in giving birth to their own understanding.

HELLO
MY NAME IS CHAPTER,

twenty-nine

Are you willing to go on a listening expedition?

The secret to growing bigger ears is listening for the *intangible* forces behind people's *physical* expressions.

So, as you sit down to listen to your employee, customer or spouse, I want you think of yourself as an archaeologist. Prepare yourself to dig deep. And be on the lookout for the four intangible forces of listening:

1. THEIR CORE.
   a) **Listen for what they value.** Something they stand for.
   b) **Listen for the appearance of vision and purpose.** Something that aligns them.
   c) **Listen for what makes issues important in their lives.** Something that drives them.

   ASK YOURSELF: What is this person (really) committed to, after all?
   ASK YOURSELF: What values are at work here?

2. THEIR PASSIONS.
   a) **Listen for what someone treasures.** Something they'd die for.
   b) **Listen for what makes them come alive.** Something that burns deep inside.
   c) **Listen for what makes them withdraw.** Something that holds them back.

   ASK YOURSELF: What is at work here?
   ASK YOURSELF: What is emerging now?

3. THEIR EVASIONS.
   a) **Listen for resistance.** Something they back away from.
   b) **Listen for avoidance.** Something they don't want to deal with.
   c) **Listen for hesitation.** Something they're uncertain about.

   ASK YOURSELF: Where is it this person doesn't want to go?
   ASK YOURSELF: What is it the person doesn't want to deal with?

4. THEIR DANGERS.
   a) **Listen for fear.** Something that terrifies them.
   b) **Listen for self-sabotage.** Something they unconsciously inflict upon
      themselves.
   c) **Listen for imbalance.** Something that throws them out of whack.

   ASK YOURSELF: What message was sent but not spoken?
   ASK YOURSELF: What is this person's immediate experience?

5. THEIR GAPS.
   a) **Listen for cognitive dissonance.** Something that divides them.
   b) **Listen for incongruity.** Something that doesn't match up.
   c) **Listen for contradiction.** Something that seems inconsistent.

   ASK YOURSELF: What disconnect could you help this person realize?
   ASK YOURSELF: What gap can you help this person bridge?

OK, Indiana. Now that you've entered the conversation with curiosity and noticed people's intangibles tendencies, the next step is to articulate what's going on.

That means helping them connect the dots.
That means telling them what you see them doing.
That means naming things out loud to realign with them.
That means illuminating truth and helping them recognize it.
That means noticing the nuances they haven't brought into their consciousness yet.

Here are four *Phrases That Payses* to help verbalize your observations in a curious, objective and non-threatening manner:

1. **"I have an observation."** Calling your comment an observation makes it neutral. You simply say what you see. Focusing on the behavior, not the person. The best part is, nobody can dispute it because it's completely subjective.

2. **"My intuition tells me that..."** By explaining that you "sense" something – in your gut, in your heart, in your soul – your comment immediately becomes neutral and irrefutable. What's more, speaking from intuition shows that you're truly listening with *your* heart and from *your* core.

3. **"That statement doesn't sound consistent with your values."** The key here is to focus on the statement, not the person who made it. Doing so will automatically cause someone to stop, recognize their cognitive dissonance and reassess their behavior.

4. **"I'm curious about that line of thinking..."** This statement is observational and focused on the thought, not the *thinker*. Also, this language reinforces the intitial goal of "entering the conversation with curiosity."

REMEMBER: Listening is Archaeology.

It's about entering the conversation with curiosity.
It's about noticing people's intangible tendencies.
It's about excavating and illuminating truth.

Put on your Fedora and start digging!

HELLO
MY NAME IS CHAPTER,
thirty

What are the two simple words that INSTANTLY make you a great listener?

Listening, as a practice, is both simple and complex.

For example, when you start getting into stuff like diminishing emotional reactivity, creating a safe space to share, responding instead of reacting, listening behind/between people's words, asking strategic questions and avoiding conversational narcissism, it can seem overwhelming.

Which is understandable. After all, listening is probably the most important thing we do.

Hell, it's the ONLY thing we do more than breathing.

But, I imagine you want answers NOW. You don't care about all that philosophical and psychological crap about honoring the other person's Truth and mindfully responding to their immediate experience.

You just want to be a better listener, TODAY.
You just want people to perceive you as a better listener, TODAY.

In that case, here are the two simple words that INSTANTLY make you a better listener:

Take notes.

That's it.
That's everything.
That's all you need to know, that's all you need to practice.
Taking notes pretty much summarizes every important lesson about listening.

For example:

Taking notes is proof.
That you're actually interested.
That you're actually paying attention.
That you're actually receiving the message.
That you're actually making an attempt to understand (not just) what they're saying;
but also what they're trying to communicate.

LET ME ASK YA THIS: How will people know when you're (really) listening to them?

Taking notes keeps you mindful in the conversation.
Dancing in the moment.
Honoring their immediate experience.
Giving people all of your energy and focus, right NOW.
Acknowledging someone's rising thoughts and feelings.
Partnering with the other person in their discovery process.
Practicing your noticing skills each time you jot something down.

LET ME ASK YA THIS: What will keep your listening posture stable?

Taking notes honors someone's thoughts.
Because they're worth capturing.
Because they're worth considering.
Because they're worth sharing with someone else in the future.
Because they're worth saving and revisiting for further contemplation.

LET ME ASK YA THIS: How are you silently complimenting people?

Taking notes is respectful.
As if to silently say, "Man, what a great idea! I gotta write that down…"
As if to silently say, "Ooh! Great word. I'm gonna have to Google that later…"
As if to silently say, "Wow. That was a powerful question. I need to remember that…"
As if to silently say, "Hmm. Good suggestion. Never thought of it that way. I'll look
into it tomorrow…"

LET ME ASK YA THIS: What are your nonverbal behaviors accidentally communicating?

Taking notes reinforces openness.
Because you allow people to see how they affect you.
Because you allow people to experience that they can change your mind.
Because you allow people to come back to you in the future with their ideas.

LET ME ASK YA THIS: How are you reinforcing your openness?

Taking notes increases someone's self-esteem.
You make them think, "He wrote that down? Sweet!"
You make them think, "Wait, did I just say something good?"
You make them think, "Wow. Maybe I'm smarter than I thought…"
You make them think, "Good. Looks like he might actually buy that book I recommended…"

LET ME ASK YA THIS: How are you making people feel essential?

OK! Now that you understand the simple, two-word secret for INSTANTLY becoming a better listener, here are several note-taking practices you can implement TODAY as you grow bigger ears:

1. **Keep a Conversation Log.** Buy a small notebook JUST for listening notes. (I highly suggest Moleskine.) Keep it handy for lunches, meetings, coffee conversations or other listening venues. This running log of various ideas and thoughts will not only keep you organized; but also come in handy as a resource. That way, during Thursday's conversation with Angela, you can easily and quickly refer back to Monday's conversation with Randy. And the best part is, when Angela notices that you've been taking notes during ALL your conversations, it will reinforce your consistency as a good listener. *What did you write today?*

2. **Don't over-write.** If you don't write it down, it never happened. Ever. For that reason, taking notes is crucial for capturing key ideas. At the same time, however, make sure to allow people's words to profoundly penetrate you. If someone makes a powerful point, before fumbling around to snag your pen, pause for a moment. Let the pearl sink. Then, once it travels from your head down to your heart, capture it. In the words of Don Henley, "What the heads makes cloudy, the heart makes very clear." *Did you really, truly, deeply understand what this person just said?*

3. **Put your pen down between notes.** This is an easy way to avoid overwriting. Kind of like resting your fork on your plate after each bite to avoid overeating. Also, this practice keeps you focused on the present

moment. Think about it: If you're listening to someone, pen in hand like a literary gunfighter, your anticipation blocks mindfulness. Careful there, Tex! *Is your pen destroying your Now?*

4. **Ask them to repeat it.** If needed, pause the conversation to gain clarification on someone's thoughts before writing them down. This demonstrates your desire to clearly understand their point. It also gives them a chance to rephrase, repeat or retweak their original idea, making it as strong as possible. Try *Phrases That Payses* like, "Wait, what was that again?" "Ooh! That's good. Can you repeat that?" "How do you spell that?" or "Hang on, let me get that down." *Are you asking for clarification?*

5. **Watch the angle of your paper.** Sometimes you don't want people to see the notes you're taking – either at all, or not until you're done listening to them. The danger is that they may become self-conscious, distracted or offended by your scribblings. Even if that wasn't your intention. So, the call is yours. It depends on the situation, the type of person and topic(s) at hand. For example, when I'm casually having lunch with a colleague of mine, brainstorming about any number of random topics, I usually keep my Conversation Log open and on the table. When I'm in a business coaching session with a client, focusing on a special improvement for their business, I tend to keep the paper to myself for the duration. Then, I later summarize the key points of the discussion in a follow-up email. *Is there anything on my notes that I'd be afraid to share with the speaker?*

6. **Turn the Tables.** Here's a fun practice. When you're finished with the conversation, or when the other person is finished with the bulk of their talking, turn your notes upside down. Let them see everything you wrote. If you want, just sit in silence as they observe what YOU observed about them and then wait for their response. This is a powerful exercise, when done with right person at the right time. Now, if that's a little too transparent for your liking, you might also consider turning your notes upside down and using them more as a visual aid for your summary. *How radically honest are you willing to be?*

7. **Follow up.** After the conversation is over, email the person. If possible, later that hour. If that's a stretch, shoot for later that day. Either way, thank them for the meeting, for sharing and for letting you listen. Then, copy your notes. Either write a bullet point summary reviewing key points, or, simply highlight one or two memorable insights from the meeting. *How are you reinforcing your bigger ears?*

So, there it is.

Everything you need to know about listening summarized in two words: Take notes.

It's proof. It keeps you mindful in the conversation. It honors someone's thoughts. It's respectful. It increases someone's self-esteem.

... meet you wherever you are.

No judgments. No evaluations. No appraisals. No worries. That's the way I feel when I hang out with my friend Dr. Tom Lipsitz. As a veteran shrink, he's seen just about everything. There's no problem you can bring to him that he hasn't been exposed to before. Now, that doesn't mean he has the answers to everything. But it DOES mean that he (1) listens attentively, (2) meets you wherever you are. Whew.

Here are six ways you can start LIVING this attribute today:

1. **One word: "Wow."** It's neutral, empathetic, non-judgmental and emotionally unreactive. It buys you time, helps maintain composure and creates space in the conversation.

2. **Articulate what's occurring.** Verbalize your observations. Dance in the moment. Respond to someone's immediate experience.

3. **Create a comfortable climate.** Honor people's feelings. Acknowledge rising thoughts. This creates a safe container in which the other person can share.

4. **Learn to be open to people you don't approve of.** I'm not accusing you of being a finger-wagging monument of judgment. Still, each of us needs to confront our prejudices and honestly ask, "What type of people am I offended by?" Remember: The awareness of your intolerance is the first step to overcoming it. My challenge to you is to learn how to play two games: (1) "Let's See How Many People I Can Talk To Today That I Don't Approve Of," and (2) "How Much Would I Have To Learn About These People To Reverse My Disapproval Of Them?" Sure, it sounds kind of silly. But that's the point. This reminds me of Herbert Leff's book, *Playful Perception,* where he suggests you regard whatever you're doing as a game. It adds a childlike sense of playfulness and adventure to whatever you're engaged in. *What invisible walls have you built? What is preventing you from, or making it hard for you to be open TO this person? What values do you hold that could influence your response to this person?*

5. **Meet people where they are.** No judgments. No evaluations. No appraisals. *That's approachable.* And, I know: "Not judging people" is easier said than done. Fine. Try this: Articulate what's occurring. Say what you see. Verbalize your observations. Respond to someone's immediate experience and dance in the moment with language like, "I noticed," "It looks like," and "I have an observation."

   Doing so helps you observe without accusing; insinuate without imposing and describe without prescribing. What's more, "saying what you see" is objective, non-judgmental, non-comparison based and emotionally unreactive. It's a statement of observation. An impartial piece of feedback that doesn't challenge someone's character or attitude, it simply meets them where they are. *What is this person experiencing because of what is happening? How is it possible that this person could think or behave in this way? And under what circumstances would it make perfect sense to do so?*

6. **Show people that their feelings are legitimate.** Avoid phrases like, "You don't really feel that way," "Oh, don't say that," or "You're making too much of a fuss about this." They come off as insincere and patronizing. And while you may THINK you're listening, you're actually doing more damage than if you had said nothing.

   I've dubbed these rote responses "You're Not Helping Phrases." Because that's exactly what they do – **detract from the effectiveness of your listening practice**. And especially when you're dealing with a person who's upset, angry, suffering or highly emotional, you want to respond as genuinely as possible.

   Consider saying, "You have a right to feel that way," "I would be frustrated too," or "It's OK to be upset." Remember: People are entitled to whatever feelings arise. Your challenge is to honor their current experience. So, watch your words. Regulate your rote responses. Steer clear of platitudes, minimizers, empty promises, shorthand listening techniques and false empathy. Because the last thing you want someone to think is, "Yeah, you're NOT helping." *How are you showing people that their feelings are legitimate? What if you saw everyone as important? And what needs to be developed in you to better handle your judgment of others?*

LET ME ASK YA THIS: How are you meeting people where they are?

How are you building a reputation as an askable person?

"Nobody ever comes up to me. Nobody ever asks any questions. What's WRONG with these people?

POSSIBLE ANSWER: Nothing.

Maybe it's YOU.

Maybe the reason nobody ever asks you any questions is because **you're NOT perceived as an Askable Person.**

Whoa. There's a counterintuitive thought. *Being Askable.* Huh.

SO, HERE'S THE SECRET: Forget about "getting" people to ask questions. Instead, identify and embody the attributes of Askable People, and the rest will fall into place.

See, whether you're a manager, executive, teacher, counselor, parent – or hold any other type of leadership position (ahem, that's ALL of us) – your approachability is a function of your ASK-ability.

Today we're going to explore a list of 29 Ways to Build Your Reputation as an Askable Person:

1. **Acceptance.** Recognize that someone has an opinion, even though it may not be your own. You don't have to agree. You don't have to disagree. Just honor it. Honor = Respect = Trust = Willingness to Ask More Questions. Otherwise you'll start to resemble Dilbert's Boss, whose management strategy is, "I'm not going to comment – I'll just look at you until you agree with me." *What is your ego having a hard time accepting?*

2. **Acknowledge the discomfort.** That's where the difficulty comes from. That's why people are hesitant to approach you: The topic makes them feel uncomfortable. You need to saddle up on that white elephant and move on. **REMEMBER:** No Conflict = No Avoidance. *What immediate preoccupation do you need to disarm?*

3. **Assuming blocks openness.** *She's too young to talk about this … He's too old to address this issue … They're not ready to deal with this yet … Really?* According to whom? *Your ego? Your insecurity? Google?* Look. Stop justifying. That attitude will seep into your words and actions and, as a result, people won't want to approach you with their questions. *What lies are your assumptions guarding?*

4. **Be wrong more.** Frequent wrongness demonstrates vulnerability, honesty and humanity. That's the kind person you want to ask questions to because, similar to yourself, he doesn't have all the answers. *When was the last time you said, "I don't know"?*

5. **Body cancels mouth.** People don't just learn from what you say, but how you BEHAVE and react to situations. That's why it's easier to tell the truth. Because you body language might rat you out. *What do people hear when they listen to what you do?*

6. **Create a Question Friendly Environment (QFE.)** A safe space. A non-threatening atmosphere where people (1) feel comfortable, and (2) feel like they have permission to ask anything that's on their minds. I don't have the space to write more than that, so here's a more detailed examination on creating a question friendly environment. *How do you define the atmosphere needed to ask an answer people questions successfully?*

7. **Dig deeper.** If you can tell that someone HAS a question, but isn't asking, trying asking yourself: *What is behind their reluctance?* Maybe they don't want to look stupid. Maybe they don't want to appear in need of help or risk ridicule and rejection. Maybe they don't want to hold up the discussion/meeting/class. Maybe they fear making a big mess and getting in trouble. Maybe they haven't discovered a safe place to be vulnerable. Maybe they think it's the wrong time to ask. Maybe they think the answer will be threatening. Maybe they think their questions aren't good questions. They were ridiculed when they questioned in the past. The list goes on and on. Get to know it. *Why might your people NOT ask questions?*

8. **Do your research.** Being informed gives you confidence and, therefore, lowers your level of discomfort in an interaction. And, because emotions are contagious, this lowers the other person's level of discomfort as well. My suggestion: Make a list called, "101 Questions My (x) Will Probably Ask Me." (The "x" in that equation stands for your peeps, i.e., students, employees, children.) *How much time do you spend preparing to listen?*

9. **Don't act embarrassed.** If someone asks you a question about a potentially uncomfortable topic (sex usually does the trick) don't try to diffuse the discomfort by making a joke out of it. That tactic only works in reverse and makes the conversation more uncomfortable. Instead, work on your poker face. Honor their question despite the fact that you might be giggling like a little schoolgirl on the inside. This form of openness will show the Asker that it's both acceptable and comfortable to discuss such issues. *Does your immature reaction to a word like "penis" prevent people from EVER asking you another question again?*

10. **Don't ask, "Why do you want to know?"** First of all, never begin a question with the word *why*. It immediately puts people on the defensive and forces them to justify their question. Secondly, the motivation behind the question isn't as important as your willingness to open a dialogue about the question. Third, if you're respectful, accepting and understanding, don't worry. The "why" be revealed to you at the right time. *What words govern your questions?*

11. **Don't be too busy to explain.** This communicates two messages to the other person: (1) My time is more valuable than yours, and (2) Your question is not important. Suggestion: Stop whatever you're doing and give yourself fully to the other person. Or, if they catch you off guard, book "blank time" in your schedule. *How many important conversations does your busyness prevent from ever occurring?*

12. **Don't dodge difficult issues.** Similar to your ability to handle good news/bad news and positive/negative feedback, also practice handling easy/difficult issues. Both are equally important and require your attention. Even if you don't have an answer, by responding with early intervention, you solve small problems before they snowball into big problems. This also proves to the other person that every difficult situation is NOT a crisis. *What questions are people afraid to ask you?*

13. **Don't laugh.** In almost every episode of *The Office*, Michael Scott will respond to crazy questions by laughing hysterically or degrading the asker.

This instantly shuts down the communication channel and destroys the desire for future encounters. So, similar to "embarrassing" questions, also learn to hold your poker face when you're asked a question that's completely illogical. Treat all questions with deep democracy. And don't laugh at irrational inquiries. Even when you're convinced the person should be locked up in a mattress-lined cell. *Why are you laughing?*

14. **Don't pretend you don't know.** First of all, people can tell. You're not that good of a liar. Secondly, skirting the issue only makes people more reluctant to ask questions in the future. Thirdly, bad advice and/or failure to communicate leads to uninformed choices, which leads to more work for you down the line. Try saying, "I don't know, but I can find out…" or "Let's go google that together." *Are willing to expose your ignorance?*

15. **Don't start talking non-stop.** That's a reaction, or a reflex. You need to respond, which is a choice. Make sure you're only talking about 30% of the time. Seek to monopolize the listening. Here's a good test: If the other person finishes their meal before you, you weren't listening enough. Or they eat too fast. *Are you vomiting or listening?*

16. **Four words: "I told you so."** This sentence – or any permutation thereof – discontinues communication and makes people start wondering why they even bothered to ask you. Look. People don't need to be reminded how badly they screwed up. The need to be reassured that you're going to (1) love them when they DO screw up, (2) help them prevent the same mistake from being made again, and (3) partner with them to brainstorm lessons learned from those mistakes. *Are you giving people permission to fail?*

17. **Give Askable Reminders.** Make it a point to tell people (employees, customer, kids, whomever) that you're available if they have any questions or problems – no matter how tough they may be. It's unwise to assume people feel comfortable seeking you out on the difficult issues. Good verbiage: "What questions do you have?" versus "Do you have any questions." *How are you reinforcing your askablity?*

18. **Give yourself permission to feel uncomfortable.** So, it's a touchy subject – fine. Deal with it. You never learn when you comfortable anyway. My suggestion: Channel that discomfort into your breathing or your enthusiasm for the person who asked the question. Don't try to conceal it, or it will find a home somewhere in your body. *Are you willing to stick yourself out there?*

19. **Go deeper anyway.** Be willing to keep talking until they're satisfied with your answer. Let what you say have an impact on them. Patiently let the pearl sink. Allow your words to profoundly penetrate them. This practice respects their speed of discovery and encourages them to come back to you with question in the future. On the other hand, if you explain something too quickly – via your head, not your heart – the other person's level of understanding will resemble the digestive ability of Cookie Monster: All chewing, no swallowing. (Ever notice how he never actually eats any of those cookies? Weird.) *How are you speaking to people where they are?*

20. **Lay a foundation of affirmation.** If you want people to come to you and come BACK to you with their questions, respect and trust MUST come first. Here's why. Acknowledgement is a universal human need. So, listening is initially about affirmation. Making people feel (not just) valued, validated and important; but ESSENTIAL. Suggestion: Always prime your responses with, "Great question!" or "Wow, that's a very intelligent question." Make the question-asker feel smart for asking, no matter what the question. *How early are you complimenting people?*

21. **Lectures lose people.** When someone asks you a question, remember these tenets: No advice. No fixing. No platitudes. No "shoulds." *Just cut to the chase. Just give people the meat.* Otherwise you'll make the person instantly regret approaching you with a question and therefore less likely to do re-approach the future. Here's the secret: Back and forth. Like a ping-pong match. An answer here, an answer there. Share values without preaching. Establish gentle flow. **REMEMBER:** If they don't come to you, they will seek answers elsewhere. Possibly from total idiots, or, worse yet, The Internet. *Anyone? Anyone? Bueller? Bueller?*

22. **Practice receiving good AND bad news equally.** Otherwise you will scare people. And they'll assume the only time they can ever approach you is when their ideas are positive. As such, your unapproachable appearance will stop question asking in its tracks. *Are you willing to suspend your judgment and evaluation of what people tell you until you've taken adequate time to process their information?*

23. **Respect confidentiality.** Let them know the question is between the two of you. Or, if anonymity is optional, allow people to write their questions on index cards and turn them in. This enables shy people to speak up because their name isn't on the line. *Do people trust you NOT to be a blabbermouth?*

24. **Seek extreme clarity.** Ask people to clarify their question EVEN when you think you understand. Then, wait until you fully understand the question fully before you answer. Don't view other people's speech as a tedious interruption of the flow of your own ideas. **REMEMBER:** You rarely hear people complain, "Damn it! I wish you wouldn't have been so clear in your answer!" *How is what (you think) you know thwarting what you need to hear?*

25. **Turn the table.** Consider how YOU would feel asking such question. Or, think about how you DID feel when you asked that same question. Go back in time. Awareness of your own attitudes, values and tendencies is necessary before you can effectively communicate with others. *How can your past make you more Askable?*

26. **Unconditional positive regard.** If you log on to the very cool parenting website, www.advocatesforyouth.com, you'll find a helpful piece on being an Askable Parent. It suggests following: "Don't withdraw love or support if what is asked is inappropriate or disappointing." Now, even if you're not a parent, the lesson is still applicable: Love people anyway. There's no such thing as a stupid question, only stupid people who don't ALLOW questions. *What types of questions piss you off?*

27. **Validate their feelings.** Never say, "You don't really feel that way." Everyone is entitled to whatever feelings arise. You need to honor whatever surfaces. It's like in *A League of Their Own* when manager Tom Hanks yells, "Are you crying? There's no crying! There's no crying in baseball!" Wrong response. Tell people they perfectly deserve to feel the way they do. This is another way to lay a foundation of affirmation. *What feelings are you not allowing people to have?*

28. **Welcome criticism and praise equally.** Learn to respond to positive AND negative questions in a supportive, helpful and non-emotionally reactive way. Otherwise people either (1) only ask easy, positive questions, or (2) not ask any questions at all. *How open are you to questions that reveal your screw-ups?*

REMEMBER: The reason people aren't asking you questions (might) have nothing to do with them.

It might have more to do with your Askability, or lack thereof.

So, forget about "getting" people to ask questions. Instead, I challenge you to identify and embody the attributes of Askable People, and let the rest follow suit.

Any questions on that?

Are people coming to you for help?

If not, try this ...

1. **Begin with a willingness to find answers.** Sadly, not everybody does. Not everybody is interested in taking the time to find answers to the questions they've been asked. Mainly because their ego won't let them. So, there's an attitude of curiosity and openness that MUST underscore your askability. Otherwise people will perceive you as someone who isn't interested in expanding his worldview. Someone who's too set in his ways. Never willing to change. Never willing to let new ideas enter his mind. And rarely interested in considering questions that challenge his point of view. This perception stops questions in their tracks, preventing you from uncovering the key issues in the lives of those you serve. *Do you WANT to find answers? What answers are you terrified of discovering? And if you set aside your ego and opened yourself to being changed, how much stronger would your organization become?*

2. **Don't force solutions**. While the willingness to find answers is essential to your askability, remember that you can't force it. Especially when the answer isn't immediately clear. Doing so only works in reverse. And any time you try to instantly compartmentalize everything that enters into your mindspace, key ideas often get overlooked. So, here's the secret: Don't be afraid to bookmark. If someone's question is (currently) unanswerable, try one of the following responses:

    -   "Great question! And you know, I have absolutely NO idea. So, let me think about that for a while. Can I email my answer to you by the end of the day?"

- "I would need to know more information about (x) to make an informed decision. If I went and did some research, when would be a good time to get back to you with my answer?"

- "I'm not sure. And because I'd rather not answer at all than try to answer poorly, would it be cool we continued this conversation after I've had some time to think about your important question?"

These types of responses reveal your imperfect humanity. They demonstrate honesty and a willingness to learn. Most importantly, they honor, affirm and respect the question AND the questioner. This assures two things: (1) You will have enough time and resources to find the best answer, and (2) People will come back to you with questions in the future. *Are you daring to be dumm? Are you fitting people's unique needs or trying to prescribe them a packaged answer? And do you possess enough self-control to NOT answer a question until you're ready?*

3. **Make passion palpable.** Not about the answer, necessarily, but passionate about the idea of answering the person, himself. After all, answers are overrated. What's more important is the search. What the answer points to. And what the process of discovery helps the other person become. See, askable people are excitable people. They love questions, they revel in curiosity and they value strategic thinking. Do that, BE that, and your positive emotions will instantly transfer to the asker. *Are you passionate about questions? What discovery process are you leading people through? And how are you transferring your love to others?*

4. **Practice psychological safety.** Another reason people shrink from asking questions is because they fear that their questions (and the answers TO those questions) will later be revealed publicly. That's why comfort, safety and in many cases, confidentiality, is HUGE for being askable. My suggestion is to build a Question Box. Not a Suggestion box, a Question Box. This keeps it informal, anonymous and organized. *How psychologically safe do people feel around you? What fears about questioning are your people plagued by? And how could you introduce anonymity into the conservation?*

5. **Be willing to share information**. Which means you can't maintain a monopoly on information. Knowledge hoarders are company hurters. Don't come across as someone who has a sense of scarcity. Share LOTS of relevant answers without the fear that it would reduce your perceived value. *What did you write today? Whom did you share it with? And what secrets are you afraid to tell?*

6. **Advice is the enemy.** People don't want advice. They want feedback. They want answers. They want you to listen. Advice creates defensiveness. And it's rarely followed because it's usually delivered from an assumed position of superiority. So, make sure NOT to say, "Can I give you some advice?" or the dreaded, "Here's a friendly piece of advice…" This immediately lowers your askability. Instead, ask your people, "How do you want to be listened to?" or "Do you want me to just listen to what you have to say or do you want my input?" *Are you a disrespectful dispenser of advice? What type of information do you answer with? And how could you respond to people's questions in a way that levels the playing field?*

7. **Thank the asker.** After a conversation in which people DID ask you questions, follow up via email, text, handwritten letter, etc., with an expression of gratitude. Thank people for courageously asking. Thank people for their specific questions. And thank people for honoring you with their openness. This lays a foundation of affirmation AND subtlely reminds people that they can comfortably and confidently return to you with questions in the future. *Do you thank people for their questions? Do you send people emails with the notes you took? And what would happen to your askability if you combined it with affirmation and gratitude?*

8. **Become perceived as a problem solver.** That means be a resource for people. For example, the aforementioned Arthur, my mentor, never fails to live this strategy. Whenever I approach him with a question, he always concludes his answer by whipping out his Blackberry and saying, "Here, I want you to write this down." And Arthur will help you populate a list – right then and there – of the people you need to connect with. Or books you need to read. Or websites you need to visit. Problem solved! *What resources do you offer people? When you don't know the answer, where do you send your asker? And wouldn't it be great if everyone who asked you questions could walk away with tangible resources to get more answers?*

9. **Help people process their answer.** Finally, once you've given people your answer, try this: Pause. Sit quiet. Build space into the conversation so your words can profoundly penetrate people. Then, help them process by answering any follow-up questions, silly as they may sound. Also, if you're taking notes, consider emailing those ideas to your Asker later on that day. This might help them visualize the conversation so they can more effectively find solutions.

10. **Dare to be asked more**. If you've ever done Q & A during a presentation, TV spot, radio interviews, or a public press conference, you certainly recognize the risk in making yourself more askable. After all, it IS a form of

sticking yourself out there. And so, notwithstanding the discomfort that's required, being askable begins with your attitude. It's about opening yourself to the possibility of being vulnerable, being wrong, and, in some cases, looking like a complete idiot. Speaking of idiots, take Sarah Palin. During the 2008 Presidential Election, she was reluctant to do almost ANY public interview. Meanwhile, opposing VP Candidate Joe Biden was everywhere. *TV. Radio. Print. Town Hall Meetings.* If you had a question, Joe would be happy to answer. Palin, on the other hand, was completely unaskable. And I wasn't surprised that the Obama campaign crushed her and John McCain. Now, I'm no political analyst, so I'm not going to make any gross assumptions. But if I had to make an educated guess as to what made Sarah Palin such an unaskable person, I'd say it's because she's never "dared to be asked more." Either that, or the fact that she was a colossal redneck bimbo moron. *Do you dare to be asked more? Are you willing to stick yourself out there? And if you were running for VP, how many interviews would YOU turn down?*

11. **An answer for one is an answer for all.** People – especially students – will shy away from asking questions because they don't want to hold up the discussion. (Especially if recess, pizza or the end of class is rapidly approaching.) Students also don't ask because they assume everyone else in the room already understands everything. However, in many classroom settings, this isn't always the case. My mentor and former high school English teacher, Mr. Jenkins, practiced an effective strategy for overcoming this fear. "I always encouraged my students NOT to approach my desk with questions, but rather, to ask me from their seats. That way, ALL the students in the class would hear the answer – including the ones who were too shy to raise their hand." What's more, this approach also helped saved time since multiple students usually pose similar questions. As my yoga instructor always says, "An answer for one is a an answer for all." *What assumptions could you dispel in your classroom? How could you kill two stones with one bird? And how much time would you save if you addressed questions communally?*

12. **Disarm immediate preoccupations.** The challenge is, many people associate question asking with conflict. So, the silent dialogue becomes: "*Asking questions means rocking the boat, which means questioning the status quo, which means making a big mess, which means getting in trouble. Better keep quiet during the meeting…*" For that reason, your goal is to make sure your people know that their answers won't be used against them. That anytime is the right time to ask. That asking questions isn't a threat to formality or a violation of the chain of command. And that when you ARE asked

questions, that you don't feel like you're being interrogated. *Who's terrified to ask you questions? When is the feeling of formality preventing your people from communicating freely and honestly? And is the status quo REALLY that important to you?*

13. **Be more informative.** Without overwhelming people with your knowledge, provide as much information as you can give AND as much as the context will allow. Think meat, not carbs. And if your asker is taking notes, that means you're doing something right. If your asker is checking their text messages or flipping through pictures of their pet ferret, you're doing something wrong. *How informative are you? How much meat are you giving people? And when you talk, do people write things down?*

14. **Help people process their questions.** My mentor, Arthur, is an expert at this practice. He's a consummate counterintuitive thinker. So, when you ask HIM a question, he often responds (not) with an answer, but with a challenge to your question itself. Common responses include,"Are you sure that's the right question to ask?""What's the question behind that question?" and,"I'm not sure that question is relevant – instead, what about asking yourself this…?"That's the cool part. By helping you process your own question, he opens up new worlds and new answers that you never would have discovered otherwise. *How are you questioning people's questions? What unexpected answers could you give people to challenge their thinking? And what would happen if, instead of having all the answers, you had all the questions?*

HELLO
MY NAME IS CHAPTER,

thirty-three

What's the most dangerous question any leader could ask?

"Do you have any questions?"

NEVER ask this.

Because the answer might be, "No."

At which point the conversation ends.
At which point you become less askable.
At which point you AND the other person stop learning.

HERE'S THE SECRET: The surefire way to GET anything is to GIVE that thing first.

Therefore, if you want to become more askable, try asking people some of these questions to get them to ask YOU questions in return:

1. What are your burning questions?
2. What are your questions of clarity?
3. What are your persistent questions?
4. What is the biggest question you have?
5. What question would be the answer for you?
6. What are the dominant questions of your life?
7. What questions of yours are still unanswered?
8. Where did that particular question come from?
9. What type of answers would you like from me?
10. What's the next question that wants to be asked?
11. What's on your list of questions you need to ask?

12. What thought prompted that particular question?
13. From what specific facts do your questions come?
14. What might be some sub-questions of this question?
15. What are the questions I haven't asked, but should have?
16. What questions did I not ask that you hoped I would ask?
17. What's going on deep down that made you ask that question?
18. What would it look like to know the answer to this question?
19. How can you refine your questions, given what you now know?
20. What answers have I not given you that you were hoping to get?
21. What other questions would you like to ask to help clarify your decision?
22. What is the question that if you had the answer to, you would be set free?
23. What questions must you have answered by the time the meeting is over?
24. What questions were you asking yourself before you walked in here today?
25. How do you define the atmosphere needed to ask your questions successfully?
26. What questions were you asking yourself when you first walked in here today?
27. If you were guaranteed honest answers to any three questions, who would you ask and why?
28. What questions were you hoping to God I wouldn't ask, that you've since changed your mind about?
29. If you were going to pay me $1000 an hour, what are the questions you would need to ask me get your money's worth?

Ask any of those questions, and you will instantly become more askable.
Ask any of those questions, and you will instantly open up new dialogue.

REMEMBER: Whatever you want to GET; just try GIVING that thing first.

Any questions on that?

HELLO
MY NAME IS CHAPTER,

thirty-four

How do you respond when people fall out of posture?

PICTURE THIS: You're a beginning yoga student. It's only your third class ever. The room is sweltering. Sweat pours out of your body like a carwash. Muscles you didn't even know you had ache and burn. Worst of all, your bottle of cold water is running dangerously low.

To make matters more intimidating, surrounding you are all veteran students, most of whom are contorted into pretzel-like positions you've only seen in the Olympics.

How would you feel? *Uncomfortable? Hopeless? Ready to walk out of the room?*

Me too. In fact, during my first few yoga classes, I felt all of the above.

But I'll never forget what my instructor, JJ, said me during one particular practice.

I remember experiencing a combination of exhaustion and disappointment. I just couldn't control my breathing. There was no way I could stay in the posture any longer.

So, I fell out.

Which was no big deal. Happens to everyone.

I plopped down on my mat to take a brief rest. JJ noticed, smiled, and said seven unexpected words:

"Thank you for listening to your body."

Huh.

Thank you for listening to your body? But I messed up! I fell out of posture. Why would the instructor be THANKING me? And then, as I lay there trying not to pass out from heat exhaustion, it started to made it sense...

Although everyone "falls out of posture" from time to time – in yoga or in life – NOT everyone has the experience of an instructor – a LEADER – who positively responds to them without judgment, evaluation or criticism.

JJ just as easily could have said, "Woops!" or "Ooh, tough break..." or "Scott! Get your lazy ass back in the posture!"

But she didn't. She thanked me for listening to my body.

And I never forgot that.

So, I share this story because I'm curious how YOU – as a teacher, leader, manager, helper, whatever – respond to YOUR people when they "fall out of posture."

Are you appraising or critical?
Are you constructive or harsh?
Are you directive or dictatorial?
Are you fascinated or frustrated?
Are you judgmental or thankful?
Are you descriptive or prescriptive?

These categories of responses (not reactions, but responses) dance along the fine line of approachability. The challenge is becoming aware of how your words, actions and attitudes shape the behaviors people you serve.

Let's revisit JJ's phrase – *Thank you for listening to your body* - and explore the elements behind it that make it successful:

1. **It's rooted in gratitude.** Saying thank you is a form of recognition. It demonstrates empathy and concern. What's more, it immediately puts a positive spin on an otherwise negative situation. It's the difference between, "Oh, I'm sooooo sorry!" and "Thanks for letting me know about that..."

   ASK YOURSELF: How are your words laying a foundation of affirmation and positivity?

2. **It's non-threatening and diffusing.** That means "encountering" people (which fosters awareness) as opposed to "confronting" people, (which elicits defensiveness.) It's the difference between telling an employee, "Steve! Get your butt into my office right now!" versus, "Hey Steve, I need your help..."

   ASK YOURSELF: Do your words alienate or engage? Do your words sound like suggestions or orders? Do your ideas liberate or imprison people?

3. **It's fair and unembarrassing.** Over the years, I've had yoga teachers that will straight up *humiliate* you during class. And while I "get" why they do it, I don't find that style to be particular effective. The challenge, as an approachable leader, is helping people, not correcting them. That means offering suggestions, not criticisms. And that means walking the fine line between accountability and EDIT-ability.

   ASK YOURSELF: Are you giving people permission or shutting people down?

4. **It's unexpectedly complimentary.** Whenever you attempt to help, correct or improve someone's behavior, always open with an affirmation or compliment about something they've already done correct. This paves the way with positivity and makes people more receptive to receiving feedback.

   ASK YOURSELF: What has this person done right that I could compliment first?

5. **It's based on mutual honor and respect.** When JJ said, "Thank you for listening to your body," it felt like we were having a conversation, not a lecture. So, this approach to leadership is the difference between giving people frameworks (which are flexible) as opposed formulas (which are reductive.) Think of it this way: In college, do you remember doing the bobble-head-doze-off-jolt-back-awake move during lectures? How many times did that happen during conversations?

   ASK YOURSELF: Are you giving lectures or having conversations? Do you require progress or perfection?

6. **It's responsive instead of reactive.** Reacting is a reflex; responding is a choice. As an approachable leader, if you want to monopolize the listening, don't bulldoze. Don't take over. Don't try to fix or solve. And don't add too much value to the conversation. Just dance in the moment and respond to the other person's immediate experience.

ASK YOURSELF: Is this an observation or an accusation? Is this an observation or an interpretation? And are you granting this person enough space to BE and SAY what is true?

7. **It's using non-judgmental, non-evaluative, non-critical language.** Every yoga teacher is different. Different words, different teaching style, different everything. And while I respect each instructor's unique personality, when you have a teacher that's overly critical or intimidating, your practice suffers as a result. I wonder how YOUR personality is affecting people's performance levels…

ASK YOURSELF: Is this an observation or a judgment? Are you giving advice, evaluation, or feedback? Are you informing people or controlling them?

OK, let's recap…

The phrase of the day was, "Thank you for listening to your body."

Now, unless you're a yoga instructor, I doubt you're going to say that sentence with any frequency.

On the other hand, as a manager, teacher, parent or whatever other role you find yourself in, remember the elements behind those seven words:

1. Gratitude.
2. Non-threatening and diffusing.
3. Fair and unembarrassing.
4. Complimentary
5. Mutual honor and respect.
6. Responsive instead of reactive.
7. Non-judgmental, non-evaluative, non-critical language.

Imagine what would happen to your organization if your daily leadership activities revolved around THOSE practices.

Now if you'll excuse me, I've got to get to yoga class.

I hope JJ is teaching today…

How challenging are you willing to be?

Challenged minds expand. Challenged minds create lightbulbs. Challenged minds mobilize resources.

AND HERE'S THE BEST PART: When you challenge people (mentally, that is) several cool things happen:

1. You gain clarity on their motives, intentions and beliefs.
2. They gain an opportunity to restate, reform and rethink their ideas.
3. Which catches their attention.
4. Which causes them to stop and think.
5. Which causes them to clarify their remarks.
6. Which causes the REAL motives and beliefs to surface.
7. Which causes you to better understand where they're coming from.

Here's a list of four practices to become more challenging TODAY:

1. **Exhaust people's limits.** Try pushing them a little harder. And a little harder. And a little harder. Don't kill 'em, but challenge people to create new edges for themselves. As my yoga instructor says, "Stretch their bodies and minds and souls to a point where they're not in pain; but where pain is definitely possible." *Whom are YOU stretching?*

2. **Practice negative thinking.** Posing occasional questions underscored with doubt and skepticism is a healthy way to maintain objectivity and curiosity. What's more, negative thinking - more specifically, negative questioning - is a protective measure. It's challenging, counterintuitive and gives you

permission to explore the downside. Human beings NEED to have (occasional) negative thoughts. **REMEMBER:** Doubt protects us. Doubt gives us choices. Doubt is smart.

3. **Train people's eyes.** Ever tried to show someone how to stare at a Magic Eye poster? You probably said something like, "Just relax your eyes, soften your gaze and don't look at anything particular." The same process goes for life. When you're with someone, explain your thinking process out loud as you observe. Let them hear how you process your visuals. Explain your inner monologue. Let them hear how you ask yourself questions. *Whose eyes are YOU training?*

4. **Tell people why.** Never assume anyone knows your reasoning for doing anything. So, don't DEFEND yourself; explain yourself. Make your motivations and intentions crystal clear. When you tell people why, they're more likely to (1) believe you, (2) understand you, and (3) respond TO you. *Are you constantly making people aware of your Why?*

EA Games is right: Challenge Everything. If you want to become more approachable, start by becoming more challenging.

HELLO
MY NAME IS CHAPTER,
thirty-six

How are you painting a compelling vision of the future?

1.21 GIGAWATTS!

What movie comes to mind when you hear those words?

Back to the Future, of course. Greatest movie of all time.

AND HERE'S THE SECRET: You don't need a Delorian to travel through time.

All you need is a question.

A well-timed question.
A well-crafted question.
A creativity-challenging, motivation-uncovering question.

I call these *Back to the Future Questions™*. They work for four reasons:

First, they *ENABLE* people to act as if the desired changed already occurred.

TRY THESE:
- How would you BE if you were already living your dream?
- How would the person you hope to become do what you're about to do?
- How would you BE if you were sure you were going to get what you wanted?
- How would your voice sound if you knew for sure you were going to get exactly what you wanted?

Next, they *HELP* people imagine what they need to become in order for their goals to manifest.

TRY THESE:
- What will this decision look like in 10 years?
- For your life to be perfect, what would have to change?
- What kind of person do you definitely NOT want to become?
- Is this experience helping you become the best version of yourself?
- If you pursued this dream, what would your life look like in 30 days?
- What would REAL fulfillment look like in this area if you were truly living your life purpose?

Third, they *EMPOWER* people to speak from the future, then look back to identify the steps that led there.

TRY THESE:
- How do you want the world to know you 3-5 years from now?
- What three things can you do TODAY to increase your freedom tomorrow?
- Look ahead six months: standing there, what decisions would you make today?
- What three small acts you could take today to prepare for the life or work that you'd like?
- What steps need to be taken to make you feel like you've achieved a Return on Investment from this new endeavor?
- What has to happen in the next year for us to be able to look back and say, "That was best possible use of our efforts"?

Lastly, they *INSPIRE* people to paint a compelling, detailed picture of the desired future and make meaningful strides toward it.

- What would your life look like right now if you were truly healthy?
- If everyone did exactly what you said, what would the world look like?
- What are the essential features of the world you want to live in so you can be your best?
- When you imagine living the life you want, how do you see yourself starting your day?
- What would REAL fulfillment look like in this area if you were truly living your life purpose?
- What if, overnight, a miracle occurred, and you woke up tomorrow morning and the problem was solved – what would be the first thing you would notice?

I challenge you to go back to the future TODAY. Try a few of these questions, or create list of your own questions.

Enable, help, inspire and empower people – including yourself - to discover the Gigawatts of Truth that lay within.

HELLO
MY NAME IS CHAPTER,

thirty-seven

Are you leading or coaching?

Sometimes, people don't need a leader — they need a coach. From my own experience as a business coach, I've collected a list of five practices you can be executing today.

1. **Facilitate; don't dominate.** *You need to make communication a relaxing experience, as opposed to breathing down people's necks.*

   PRACTICE: Remember to … pause. Pausing creates space, space enables clarity, and clarity eases the mind. Examples: Remember to pause before you give an answer, after you ask a question, when someone else is on a roll or after powerful insights. Then, allow people's words and ideas to profoundly penetrate you, as well as allowing YOUR words to profoundly penetrate others. Consider drawing the "pause" symbol from your remote control and stick it on the edge of your computer screen.

   LET ME ASK YA THIS: How do most people feel when they're around you?

2. **Give personal attention.** *Listening, speaking, approaching, meeting and attending to others – wherever they are – makes them feel (not just) important, but essential.*

   PRACTICE: Remember people's answers. Paraphrasing is overrated. Telling people, "So, what I'm hearing you say is…" has a tendency to sound a bit contrived, almost as if you were trying REALLY hard to look like a good listener. Like you just finished taking a Dale Carnegie Course on active listening. And the danger is, when listening is approached as a technique, it can work in reverse. Because people can smell it. So, next time you're listening to a customer or employee, try repeating their EXACT words back to them. Take notes too. I promise you: This practice will ~~show~~ prove that you were truly listening.

LET ME ASK YA THIS: What's your strategy for dancing in the moment and responding to someone's immediate experience?

3. **Provide candid feedback in a way that facilitates growth.** *Honesty, while it may hurt someone's ego, will always help their practice.*

    PRACTICE: My yoga instructor, JJ, epitomizes this skill brilliantly. She walks the fine line between honestly verbalizing her observations and helping you deepen your practice – WITHOUT making you feel like a total idiot for screwing up. For example, instead of telling her students, "If you can't do this posture," she'll say, "If this posture is not available to you." Also, if you fall out of the pose she'll say, "Thank you for listening to your body," as opposed to, "Ginsberg! You pathetic maggot! Put down that water and get your sweaty ass back onto the mat!"

    LET ME ASK YA THIS: What actions are you taking to build a reputation as a dispenser of truth?

4. **Lead people according to their unique needs.** *Putting people in boxes isn't very productive, nor does it relate to them individuals.*

    PRACTICE: Every time you encounter someone, you unconsciously project (via your attitude, verbiage, body language, etc.) your answer to this question: *What do you see when you see people?* So I challenge you and your colleagues to spend fifteen minutes writing out your answer to that question. Then, share you answers with each other. Do this exercise every six months. That will align your behaviors with people's unique needs and help you attend to them as human beings, not as "ENFJ's."

    LET ME ASK YA THIS: Are you typing or harmonizing?

5. **Deliver specific and constructive feedback via coaching.** *People are more receptive to "being coached" than "being managed."*

    PRACTICE: Every once in a while, colleagues or clients of mine will ask me to help them edit their book manuscripts. Now, personally, I'd rather paper cut myself to bloody pulp then do ANY sort of editing. Not my thing. Not to mention, I'm not very good at it. Especially for work that's not my own. *Blech*. But, sometimes you gotta help your friends out. So, let me share my simple two-step process for editing on the rare occasions when I've accepted such assignments. And I want you to think about how you could apply this process to your own coaching practice: *First, tell people what you liked. Second, tell people what you'd like to see more of.* That's it. That's editing. That's coaching. And I'm challenging you to think about how you could manage less and coach more.

LET ME ASK YA THIS: Are you asking questions or hurling demands?

How do most people feel when they're around you?

... make room for ignorance

There's nothing wrong with *being* ignorant, only staying ignorant.

I learned this from Carol, owner of *Bikram Yoga St. Louis,* which I've happily mentioned several times so far in this book.

Whenever she has beginners, newbies and first timers in the studio, she always recognizes and honors them at the beginning of class. In a non-threatening, non-putting-you-on-the spot kind of way, she reminds beginners that's it's perfectly fine to (1) not know what to do, (2) sit out if you're tired/lost, or (3) look to the veterans in the front of class for guidance and support. That way, no mater how inexperienced or ignorant you are, there's always room to grow and deepen your practice.

Here are six ways you can start LIVING this attribute today:

1. **Communicate before you have to.** Otherwise it will feel forced, superficial and therefore, ineffective. In the book *Total Life Coaching,* authors Williams & Thomas suggest that when people only communicate out of need, their need speaks louder than their words. This results in an imbalance between verbal and non-verbal expressions. (Not good.)

   Here's a goal to set for yourself: Tell the truth, tell it all and tell it now. Otherwise people will fill in the gaps with their own worse case scenarios. Even if that means saying, "Steve, I have no answer for you right now, so I promise to let you know by the end of the day." This reinforces others' involvement in the decision-making process. What's more, the speed of the response IS the response.

   Ultimately, if you learn to approach people when they don't have problems, they'll be more likely to approach you when they DO have problems. By responding with early intervention, you solve small problems before they snowball into big problems. *How could you communicate with this person despite your lack of need to do so?*

2. **Use the word "wow."** It's a neutral, versatile, empathetic, non-judgmental and emotionally unreactive term. It buys you some time, until you can define your official response. It also helps you maintain composure when presented with unexpected, difficult or crucial information. Ultimately, it creates objective space in the conversation, which grants the speaker permission to continue. *Is this really the right time to play the emotion card? What is preventing you from listening to and fully connecting with this person? And when you are emotionally involved in conversation, how well do you communicate, really?*

3. **Practice the presence.** Especially when you're listening. Focus on the breath. Focus the other person's immediate experience. Focus on how their words have an affect on you. Also, when you're not listening, you can do the same. Find a way to incorporate deep breathing into everything you do. *Is your presence calming others?*

4. **Teach only after you've listened completely.** It's respectful. It's approachable. It assures you have all the information you need. It also increases the likelihood that someone else will listen to you. Because you did it first.

5. **Practice participatory management.** Stop dominating. Stop dictating. Stop doing and saying things AT people. Try WITH them instead. They might actually listen back to you. *How are you creating an environment where healthy participation naturally emerges?*

6. **Remember people's answers.** Paraphrasing is overrated. Telling people, "So, what I'm hearing you say is…" has a tendency to sound a bit contrived, almost as if you were trying really hard to look like a good listener. Which, of course, means you weren't actually listening. Next time you're listening to a customer or employee or family member, trying repeating their exact words back to them. Take notes too. I promise you: This practice will ~~show~~ prove that you were truly listening. *How are demonstrating the size of your ears?*

LET ME ASK YA THIS: How are you making room for ignorance?

HELLO
MY NAME IS CHAPTER,

thirty-eight

What is affecting your ability to be taken seriously?

I know this guy named Dalton.

I wouldn't say we're friends, but we've met a few times. We tend to speak at some of the same conferences. And I happen to think he's pretty good, even though his style is much different than my own.

Still, I'll never forget the day when I overheard one of his audience members tell her friend, "You know, with that mullet, I've always had a hard time taking Dalton seriously."

Wow.

What about YOU? What is affecting YOUR ability to be taken seriously?

Consider these six questions to make sure people don't tune you out:

1. **What causes YOU to (not) take someone seriously?** Here's a revealing exercise you might noodle with: (1) Make a list of three people you've never taken seriously, (2) Write down what, specifically, causes you to feel that way, and (3) Ask yourself if you embody any of those attributes. Your lack of self-awareness may startle you. As Ken Shelton, founder and editor of *Executive Excellence Magazine* said, "With a little self-deception, we might believe that we are number one when in fact we're not even on the charts."

   REMEMBER: Self-awareness creates options.

2. **How might you be accidentally diminishing the perception of your expertise?** My pal Robert Bradford, founder of The Center for Simple Strategic Planning, once told me that every time you add a comma to the description of what you do, you suck a little bit more. What about you? Are you positioning yourself as an expert in seventeen different areas? Are you spreading yourself too thin? Maybe people would take you more seriously if you picked a lane.

   REMEMBER: Periods, not commas.

3. **What's your system for keeping yourself constantly relevant?** Your customers, audience members, listeners and readers want to know what you've done for them lately. They want to know what you learned yesterday. You challenge is to create a game plan that keeps new wisdom coming through a revolving door. For example, I read five books a week. That's one of the (many) ways I stay relevant.

   REMEMBER: If you're not current, you're not credible.

4. **What are you unconsciously doing that's marring your credibility?** The word "credibility" comes from the Latin *creditum*, which means, "a loan, thing entrusted to another." That's interesting. *Credibility is on loan.* Which means your credibility might take years to assemble, but only seconds to annihilate. So, I'd spend some time thinking about situations in which your perception of other people's credibility diminished. Then ask yourself if you're mirroring any such behaviors in your own world.

   REMEMBER: Credibility diminishes quickly.

5. **How unquestionable is your knowledge base?** When it comes to your area of expertise, you need to be able to talk forever. Period. In order to make that happen, my first suggestion is to make sure that everything you know is written down somewhere. Everything. After all, if you don't write it down – it never happened. Plus, when you write it down, you make it sound. My second suggestion is that you read 500 books about your topic. Simple as that. Thirdly, constantly search for and dissect new dimensions to your area of expertise. This enables you to answer any question, any time, about any area of your subject.

   REMEMBER: Experts charge more.

6 **What are you doing, saying or being that's making you unlistenable?**
I've written extensively on the topic of being a listenable leader and becoming the most listenable person you know. And here's what I've learned: *Listenable people are taken seriously*. Period. So, here's a rapid list of practices for doubling your listenability: Listen first. Pamper the short-term memory. Be funny early and often. Articulate strategy and ideas in plain language. Create a zone of respect around you without being overbearing. When it's a technical matter, (still) speak English. Communicate reasons for changes and decisions. And of course, always speak with MCI, or Meaningful Concrete Immediacy.

REMEMBER: Listenable people win.

In summary, let's look to Google for a final picture of what it looks like when people don't take you seriously. I did several searches on the following phrase: *"I can't take her/him/them seriously because…"*

The results were astounding. And as you read them, I challenge you to think one last time about what might be causing people to not take YOU seriously:

"I can't take her/him/them seriously because…"

- "…They can't walk their talk." *Is your integrity intact?*
- "…He tries too hard to be evil." *Are you overexerting?*
- "…There's nothing real here at stake." *Are you relevant?*
- "…I'm so used to them another way." *Are you a chameleon?*
- "…I feel she's too preachy these days." *Are you Billy Graham?*
- "…They don't take their work seriously." *Are you serious enough?*
- "…They take themselves TOO seriously." *Are you self-important?*
- "…They change their minds about everything." *Are you wishy-washy?*
- "…We are too busy laughing at their stupidity." *Are you an idiot?*
- "…They are so obviously just seeking attention." *Are you waiting to be noticed?*

"I can't take her/him/them seriously because…"

- "…She, herself, has done worse things than me." *Are you a poor role model?*
- "…She looks like a guest on the Jerry Springer show." *Are you dressed professionally?*
- "…80% of the pictures out there of her have her in a bikini." *What happens when someone does a Google image search on your name?*
- "…All of the effects and style is so old-fashioned looking to me." *Are you a dinosaur?*
- "…When I listen to her try to make her points, I feel like I'm watching a PTA meeting." *Are you boring?*
- "…If they were half as smart as they claimed, they'd be able to make their points or get rich without having to hurt people." *Are you compensating?*
- "…It's just shtick, and when she actually says, "No, I'm dead serious," we still can't take her seriously because that too is just more shtick." *Do you have substance to support your shtick?*
- "…They give me powdered creamers or tiny plastic cream packets soaking in a tub of what used to be ice that's now melted into grey, dirty water that people have been dipping their dirty hands in." *Are you gross?*

REMEMBER: People won't take you seriously if they're too busy questioning you.

Especially if you have a mullet.

HELLO
MY NAME IS CHAPTER,

thirty-nine

Do people have to be careful what they say around you?

My favorite scene in *Meet The Fockers* is when Ben Stiller gets stuck baby-sitting Little Jack.

Searching for anything to keep his infant nephew entertained, Focker resorts to singing a broken version of Mockingbird:

"And if that mockingbird don't sing, Greg is gonna buy you a diamond ring … and if that diamond ring gets sold, Greg is gonna feel like a … big asshole."

At which point Little Jack replies, *"Ass … hooooole!"*

"No!" Greg exclaims. "Oh, no, you don't wanna say that word, cause that's a bad word!"

"Ass … hooooole!"

But it was too late. Little Jack instantly added that word to his vocabulary. And if you know anything about the impressionability of children, you can guess what happened next.

Little Jack just kept saying it. Over and over. Like one of those annoying green parrots at the zoo.

"Ass … hooooole!"

And, to make matters worse, the rest of Greg's family – which included Father-in-Law Robert DeNiro (yikes!) – was coming home soon. And thanks to Focker, that expletive seemed to be the ONLY word Little Jack knew.

"Ass ... hooooole!"

So, why did this happen?

Easy. That's what kids do. That's how they learn. *They imitate and repeat.* You don't have to be a parent to know that.

As so, one of the basic principles of Baby-Sitting 101 is, "Be careful what you say around them."

Hmm. Now there's an interesting concept. *Be careful what you say around them.*

I wonder what would happen if we applied that same principle to the adult world? I wonder what would happen if we stopped talking babies and start talking business?

See, there IS a direct correlation between this principle and YOUR reputation.

THINK ABOUT IT: Are you the kind of person who, when other people describe you, they have to add the warning, "You have to be careful what you say around him."

I hope not. Because if this is the reputation you've earned – intentionally or incidentally – you might have a problem. If this is the thought in people minds when they're talking about, talking to, approaching or being approached by you – you might have a problem.

Because the REAL implication of the warning, "You have to be careful what you say around him"? suggests a combination of the following perceptions:

- You're easily offended.
- You're closed-minded & judgmental.
- You violate interpersonal trust by gossiping.
- You don't give people permission to b fully truthful.
- You allow your emotions to get in the way of listening.
- You remember things and twist people's words against them.

And as a result, three dangers occur:

DANGER #1: People will be on guard around you. Tense. Self-conscious. Afraid to offend you. Walking on eggshells. Hesitant to set off your emotions.

And the mental energy they expend on those fear-based thoughts (1) robs them of their ability to be true, (2) prevents them from offering full information and (3) scares them away from sharing what's most important.

DANGER #2: Then, interactions will seem longer because people will feel uncomfortable. And interactions will end prematurely because people will just want to get the hell out of there! Ultimately, this reputation that precedes you will contaminate the space. People won't feel like it's is a safe container in which they can share.

DANGER #3: This unapproachable behavior will also prevent the possibility of making communication a relaxing experience. And the worst part is, your reputation as someone whom people have to "be careful what they say around" will stop future communication in its tracks.

"Ass ... hooooole!"

To sidestep those dangers, let's explore of six strategies for laying a foundation of approachability. When executed consistently, they will foster open, honest and complete communication with people you serve. Ultimately, they will help dispel the myth that people always have to be careful what they say around you.

1. **Establish safety early.** If confidentiality is an issue, make sure you address that right away. Try *Phrases That Payses*, like, "This is completely off the record,""This is between you, me and the stapler," or "I want you to know that nobody else is going to know about this but us."

   This lets people know they can share honestly, openly and fully with you. No holding back. No fear of being ridiculed. Just a safe space. The earlier you establish this, the more comfortable people will become around you. *How safe do people feel around you? How quickly do you create a question-friendly environment? And are you someone others can be dumb in front of?*

2. **Give people permission.** To open up. To request help. To ask question. To offer feedback. To feel vulnerable. To share victories and mistakes. To volunteer information and concerns. To discuss workplaces problems before they snowball. To comfortable and confidently be their true self.

The secret is, whatever your people need permission to do; just make sure YOU execute that action first. My suggestion: Practice radical honesty. Reveal your vulnerability. Become a living brochure of your own awesomeness. The more you practice those, the more you grant people permission to reciprocate. *What do your people need permission to do? What do your people need permission to BE? And how could you stick yourself out there FIRST to pave the way for future openness?*

3. **Share your thinking.** If people never know what's on your mind, your unpredictability will heighten their apprehension and lower your approachability. And the silent dialogue will become, *"For all I know, could be a ticking time bomb this morning! Better not say anything deep or lengthy."*

   As a result of this unapproachable pattern, your communication topics will always remain superficial with the people around you. Nobody will get to the heart of any important issues because they're holding back, unsure about how you might react. *How are you initiating movements toward people? What is causing you to be easily misunderstood? And what are you doing that prevents people from learning from you?*

4. **Become someone others could tell anything.** Here's a cool exercise: Get together with a close friend, colleague or superior. Have both people write down the name of ONE person in their lives in they feel they could tell anything. Next, ask the following questions to yourselves: Why? What are the character attributes of those people? And what, specifically, have they done in the past to earn that position in our minds?

   Then, write those attributes down on a sheet of paper. Rate yourself on a scale from 1-10 on how well you embody those attributes. Then, exchange papers and have your partner rate you on those same attributes without looking at your original score. When you're done, see how close the numbers get. You may be pleasantly surprised or unpleasantly shocked. *Are you someone others could tell anything? Who confides in you? Whom do you confide in? And how would your business change if you were perceived as someone whom others could tell anything?*

5. **Grow thicker skin.** If you're the kind of person who takes offense to everything, here's what will happen. People will start tiptoeing around you, trying their hardest not to get caught in your vortex of hypersensitivity. Then, they may purposely leave out important points just to avoid pushing your hot buttons. And all that's going to do is leave you in the dark.

My suggestion: Practice accepting opposition to your viewpoints or decisions without considering it a personal attack. Divorce your ego. Detach. And learn to treat all ideas – even the ones that embarrass or contradict you – with deep democracy.

As Dr. Robert Sutton explains in *The No Asshole Rule*, "Adopt a frame that turns your attention to ways in which you are no better or worse than other people." Or, if that doesn't help you grow thicker skin, you can always sing karaoke or participate in an open mic night. *At what point during a conversation do you usually start tuning people out? How can you apply what you're hearing, even if you've heard it before?*

REMEMBER: Be not tolerant OF or satisfied WITH interpersonal distance.

I challenge you to make a concerted effort to understand how other people experience you. I challenge you to become someone others could tell anything. And I challenge you to become known as someone around whom other people don't have to "be careful what they say."

Otherwise, your new nickname might become *HELLO, my name is "Ass … hooooole!"*

Do your employees want to murder you?

According to a 2009 study by CNN.com, nobody likes being killed. Here are four suggestions for preventing this from happening to you:

1. **Let people finish what they have to say.** *Most interruptions are derailments, and as such, most interrupters are avoided.*

   PRACTICE: On a daily basis, challenge yourself to play the game called, "Let's See How Long I Can Go Without Interrupting People." Actually keep score. See if you can beat your personal best each day. Then, every time you DO interrupt (unnecessarily, that is), drop twenty bucks in a jar. Get the whole office involved in the game. Then, at the end of month, use the money to have a BBQ. Or donate it to charity. That should puts an end to the interrupting.

   LET ME ASK YA THIS: Does your conversational narcissism irritate people?

2. **Listen with the ear of your heart, not your ego.** *Judgmental attitudes stop communication before it starts.*

   PRACTICE: Post a sticky note on your desk that reads, "Are you listening with your heart or with your ego?" This serves two purposes: (1) A visual reminder of what to listen WITH during your conversations, (2) An accountability measure to assess your listening practices after your conversations are through. Then, should you catch yourself listening more with your ego and less with your heart, here's what you do. Take ten extra minutes before clocking out to replay key conversations in your head. Then honestly ask yourself, "How would my heart have listened in that conversation if my ego wasn't engaged?

LET ME ASK YA THIS: Are you monopolizing the talking or the listening?

3. **Recognize employee contributions and ideas.** *According to Dilbert, most leaders will listen thoroughly to your input, thank you for your suggestions, and then do exactly what they planned all along.*

   PRACTICE: Just sit quiet. Your hand doesn't have to shoot up first. Next time you attend a meeting or sit on a panel, play a game called "Let See How Long I Can Go Without Contributing." This will force you to listen FIRST and hear everyone else out before stating your position. Yes, it takes self-control; but you never know – you may hear something that adds to, modifies or betters your idea.

   LET ME ASK YA THIS: Is your listening all show and no go?

4. **Remain calm when confronted with different points of view.** *The word "emotion" comes from the Latin* emotere, *which means, "to disturb."*

   PRACTICE: Take a few breaths. Recognize that someone has an opinion, even though it may not be your own. You don't have to agree. You don't have to disagree. Just honor it. Honor = Respect = Trust = Increased Willingness to Ask More Questions. Otherwise you'll start to resemble Dogbert, whose management strategy is, "I'm not going to comment – I'll just look at you until you agree with me."

   LET ME ASK YA THIS: When you are emotionally involved in conversation, how well do you communicate?

Are you monopolizing the talking or the listening?

ot)

Approachable Leaders ...

... share the spotlight.

It's one thing to shine; it's another thing to create an atmosphere where OTHERS can shine. Richard Tait, founder of *Cranium*, practices this principle daily. At a recent conference where he and I both conducted workshops, I remember him saying, "When you give each individual person a chance to shine, everybody wins." So, it's all about permission. Making people feel like it's OK to be awesome. Like it's cool to kick ass. Hooray!

Here are six ways you can start LIVING this attribute today:

1. **Three simple words.** "What about you?"

2. **Accomplishment introductions.** Without making someone feel TOO awkward, introduce them along with something they've accomplished. For example, "Carol, this is my colleague, Sasha. She recently published a photography book about her adventures in Venezuela."

3. **Make 'em shine.** In a group conversation, highlight someone's successes by saying, "Hey Courtney, didn't YOU have a lot of success with that strategy that year?"

4. **Be sensitive to other people's communication apprehension.** If someone is shy, don't fuel the fire. Humans form their identities based on how others have responded to them in the past. That's why shy people are shy people. Because other people have consistently TOLD them they were shy people.

   If you observe that a person is shy, the last thing you want to do is say, "Don't be shy!" or "Oh, are you shy sweetheart?" Big mistake. Instead, make yourself accessible outside of group situations for people who are shy in front of others. Also, as you exit conversations or meetings, remind people that they can still come to you at any time in the future with related questions or ideas, even if it's after the fact. *How do you treat shy people? Are you someone people could tell anything? And what type of person would you have to become to make even the shyest people willing to open up around you?*

5. **Communicate to people that you understand what is important to them.** Let me share four words that changed my life forever: *Nobody cares about you.* I know. It's hard to wrap your head around that. But it's true. People don't care how good you are – they care how good you're going to help them become. People don't care what you've done – they care what you've

learned, and how those lessons can help them. And people don't care if you're having a bad day – they care how you're going to help them have a better day.

Try these *Phrases That Payses* to let people know that you understand what's important to them: "I can see this is important to you," "I know how much this means to you," and "Jim, you obviously wouldn't have knocked off that jewelry store if you didn't love your wife." Also, here's another exercise that will keep you focused on whoever your "them" is. Ask yourself the following questions, each of which can be phrased for individuals or groups of people:

- What is this person's success seed?
- What is the key to this person's heart?
- Who does this person need to look good for?
- What is #1 on this person's Self Interest List?
- What does this person's self-interest hinge upon?
- Who can hurt this person the most, and how can I address that?
- What underlying objective or goal does this person's role create?

Remember: Nobody cares about you. They care about them. As my friend Robert Bradford so bluntly says, "People care about money, sex and happiness. That's about it." *Who are most of your conversations "all about"? How quickly do you invite other people to talk about their passion? If you had a stopwatch, how many seconds could you go in the conversation without talking about yourself?*

6. **Expand your openness to learning from others.** Here's a cool little strategy I've been practicing for many years. Not only does it demonstrate openness to learning form others; it also makes people feel essential. Not just important and valued – essential.

    After a lunch conversation, engaging phone call or even a round of golf with a customer, employee, whatever, send that person an email with the subject line, "11 Things I Learned from You Today." Recap some of the best "keepers" from your conversation.

    It shows you listened, it shows you care and it shows you're approachable enough to learn from anybody, anytime, anywhere. *How vulnerable are YOU willing to be? How, specifically, do show others that they've been listened to? And what would happen to your storehouse of wisdom if you allowed everyone you came in contact with to mentor you?*

LET ME ASK YA THIS: How are you unlocking people's brilliance?

HELLO
MY NAME IS CHAPTER,

forty-one

Where do you suck?

During a 2004 standup act in St. Louis, I'll never forget when Jerry Seinfeld said, "There are only two types of feedback: 'That's great!' and 'That sucks!'"

That got me thinking:

1. Would you rather have people around you pampering your ego by telling you why you're so great?

2. Or, would you rather have people around you improving your performance by telling you where you suck?

Personally, I'd prefer option #2. And here's why:

Whether the feedback comes from your family members, employees, colleagues, mentors – or even your yoga instructor – I think we have the greatest probability of getting better when we find out where we suck.

Here's a list of ways to become more coachable, more malleable and more feedbackable:

1. **Be available physically, mentally and emotionally.** *An Open Door policy only accomplishes SO much.*

   PRACTICE: Try listening (all the way through) to ideas that make you uncomfortable. Maybe because they sound crazy. Maybe because they're new and different and unexpected. Maybe because they're rooted in a different value system than your own. Whatever the case may be, just let people finish. Your patient openness will both shock people AND give them subconscious permission to open up even further. And who knows? You might even learn something new and (GASP!) change your own mind.

LET ME ASK YA THIS: Are your ears, mind and heart open too?

2. **Greet criticism with a welcoming heart.** *You need to be brave enough to find out where you suck.*

   PRACTICE: Four words: "I need your help." This is one of the most powerful phrases in any language. And it works because it's open, honest, admits vulnerability and appeals to another human being's inherent helpful nature. Commit to using this phrase at least three times a day, every day, for the next three months. (It helps to do this exercise with a partner.) Keep a journal of every time you say it. Then, hold each other accountable by revisiting your entries and experiences once a week.

   LET ME ASK YA THIS: What is your ego preventing you from learning about yourself?

3. **Open yourself to feedback without becoming defensive.** *Your ego is desperately trying to prevent new ideas from entering into your consciousness.*

   PRACTICE: Hold regular Listening Meetings. *No agenda. No structure. No nothing.* Anything goes. Just stand in front of your employees, listen and answer their questions. For sixty minutes. And I'm not talking about the pre-approved list of questions your assistant filtered before the meeting. I'm challenging you to demonstrate your vulnerability and dance in the moment. (Also, provide question notecards to make anonymity optional. That wasy, shy people will be more likely to open up.)

   LET ME ASK YA THIS: What barriers to learning have you built?

4. **Seek advice and coaching from others.** *The best leaders are lifelong students.*

   PRACTICE: Three simple words: "I don't know." Say thrice daily. It cuts down on the pressure to know everything. Plus, pretending like you DO know when you don't cracks your foundation, your integrity. It's a falsehood in your personality, and most people can see it from a mile away. Being vulnerable, on the other hand, means being secure enough to be who you are, even if who you are is wrong. What's more, in a sea of gargantuan professional egos, your vulnerability and openness to coaching will stand out as a refreshing change.

LET ME ASK YA THIS: Who's currently coaching you?

5. **Remain open to positive AND negative feedback about yourself.** Jerry Seinfeld said it best, "There are only two types of feedback: 'That's great!' or "That sucks!' Either way, when someone takes the time to offer you REAL feedback or constructive criticism, try this. Even if you disagree with it, even if you don't value it, THANK them for it. Without this expression of gratitude, you run the risk of shutting down the flow of valuable information that (could have) helped you become more effective in your role.

And often times, it's just a matter of asking. Try these *Phrases That Payses:*

- What can I do to become a better…?
- How do you perceive my expectations of you?
- Can you tell me more about what you're feeling?
- Will you give me some feedback about what I just said?
- Can you tell me specifically what I did that made you think to that?
- Will you tell me more about what you didn't like about what I said/did?
- Can you tell me about a time when it happened so I can better understand?
- How might I recognize when you have something difficult to express to me?

Also, here's an approach I've used for years to demonstrate openness to feedback about myself: "Would you be willing to share with me a list of specific points about (x)? And I request this not in a 'tell me why I'm so great' way, but rather, 'tell me what worked so I can replicate it in the future.'" Works every time!

REMEMBER: Find out where the rock created the ripple and either: 1) Throw more rocks, or 2) Stop throwing rocks all together. After all, finding out where you suck is the only way you will improve. *What is your feedback system? What types of feedback do you regularly request from others?*

How much employee loyalty are you sacrificing by being unapproachable?

ANSWER: Too much.

Whether you're a manager, team leader, CEO, executive director – or simply someone to whom others look to for guidance – I'm challenging you to melt away the layers that clog, contaminate or close off the communication channels between you and the people you serve.

NOTE: As you explore these attributes, you may find yourself saying, "Yeah, I already know that."

And if that's the case, fantastic! Just **REMEMBER:** Knowledge is overrated.

And so, the next step will be to honestly ask yourself: "Am I practicing and LIVING this attribute too?"

Let's find out…

1. **Create a zone of respect around you without being overbearing.** *Those who build credibility into everything they do are listened to.*

   PRACTICE: Beware of unspecified attribution. Delete the following vague, non-believable phrases from your vocabulary: *Studies show. Recent research proves. Scientists say. Psychologists report. Experts believe. They say. There's an old story that says. I've heard. Most people agree. It is said that. Critics say. Statistics* *show. Somebody once said. The reviews say.* Um, no, they DON'T. None of that is good enough. In a conversation. In a speech. In an article. In a presentation. You need to PROVE your point. With facts. Sources. Numbers. Dates. Otherwise people have no reason to believe you. **REMEMBER:** Credibility comes from specificity. If you can't cite a source, keep your mouth shut. Something isn't always better than nothing.

LET ME ASK YA THIS: What is preventing people from taking you seriously

2. **Eagerly pursue new knowledge, skills, and methods.** *Approachability is a function of teachability.*

PRACTICE: In the book *Counterfeit Leadership,* Ken Shelton explains, "Continuous learning is the best protection against pride. A person who is vigorously learning can't be egotistical about what he or she knows, because each increase in understanding reveals a larger area of ignorance." So, the secret to being teachable is daring to be dumm. Demonstrating a willingness to put your ego on the shelf and approach everyone and everything as your teacher, mentor and resource. Without such mental flexibility and openness, here's what happens: You stop learning, which means you stop growing, which means you start dying. *Yikes.* Not good for business.

LET ME ASK YA THIS: How many books did you read last month?

3. **Make, own and share your screw-ups.** *Approachability is a function of vulnerability.*

PRACTICE: Whether you're interacting with employees, clients, guests, attendees, colleagues, members, congregants, friends and students – even your own kids – acknowledge and embrace all aspects of who you are. Even the inadequate parts. My suggestion: *The earlier, the better.* Doing so builds a foundation of credibility and trust, plus it subconsciously grants other people permission to feel comfortable in their truth too. **REMEMBER:** Living falsehoods is EXHAUSTING. Let your mistakes speak. People will listen.

LET ME ASK YA THIS: How have you proven that you support and reward failure?

4. **Preserve people's self-esteem.** *The need to feel accepted is the driving force of their actions.*

PRACTICE: Let them know you need them. Let them know they've helped or inspired you. Offer your attention TO and acknowledgment OF their contributions to your worldview. Each of these practices can be accomplished in two words: "Take notes." Taking notes is proof. Taking notes keeps you mindful in the conversation. Taking notes honors someone's thoughts. Taking notes is respectful. Taking notes increases someone's self-esteem. Especially when you email them a copy of your notes five minutes after the conversation. Wow.

LET ME ASK YA THIS: How are you helping people fall in love with themselves?

5. **Tolerate honest mistakes as learning experiences.** *People don't need to be reminded how badly they screwed up.*

   PRACTICE: Instead, people need to be reassured that you're going to love them when they DO screw up, help them prevent the same mistake from being made again, and partner with them to brainstorm lessons learned from those mistakes. Try this. At your next meeting, go around the room and require each person to (1) share a mistake they recently made, (2) offer three lessons they learned FROM that mistake, and (3) suggest the practical application of those lessons to the other people in the room. Then, later that week, create a hard copy of all the mistakes and lessons shared during the meeting. Staple a $20 bill to it and send it to everyone who attended. And what you do is, attach a sticky note that says, "Thanks for being human!"

   LET ME ASK YA THIS: How are encouraging and rewarding mistakes?

6. **Treat people with respect and fairness, regardless of their position or influence.** *Titles are worthless labels whose sole function is to give people a reason to pigeonhole, avoid or judge you.*

   PRACTICE: Acknowledge everybody. This one shouldn't even be on my list. But, because not everybody practices this simple act of approachability, I've included it. So: Slow down. Stay present. Hold your eye contact with everyone you encounter for one additional second. ONE second. That's what Bill Clinton does. Also, see if you can acknowledge every single person you encounter for one whole day. It's harder than you think. Then again, it all depends on what you see when you see people. **REMEMBER:** Unspoken hierarchies hamper the freedom of expression and, as a result, create a distance between people.

   LET ME ASK YA THIS: What unnecessary title is preventing people from getting to know the REAL you?

REMEMBER: Employees don't care if your door is open – they care if your heart, mind and ears are open.

So, if you want to give people permission to come up TO, feel relaxed AROUND, open up WITH, comfortably walk away FROM, and confidently return TO you...

...You need to open more than just the door.

I challenge you to do THAT, and the next time your company runs a 360 evaluation of your performance, I promise you won't be taken off guard.

HELLO
MY NAME IS CHAPTER,

forty-three

What will be your legacy of openness?

What will you be remember for? What will you be remembered as? Consider these practices for leaving (and LIVING) a legacy of openness:

1. **Accept bad news without the need for sugarcoating.** That way, your people can give it to you straight. They can feel comfortable reporting negative information without the fear of being reamed by your emotional reactivity. So, if you want this to happen, you have to demonstrate that you support failure. And a great place to start is by sharing a few of your own screw-ups FIRST. Sometimes that's all the permission people need. *Do you respond well to good and bad news?*

2. **Acknowledge others' contributions to your worldview.** Let people know their thinking has affected you. Here's how: (1) Show them the notes you took when you were listening to them, (2) Tell them how you recently quoted them during another conversation, and (3) Share with them the insights you've stumbled upon after being inspired by something they said. *Who's toggling your brain?*

3. **Allow nothing to be meaningless in your sight.** Ideas. Problems. Experiences. And especially people. They're ALL good to you. They all have value. They all serve a purpose. Because your attitude is: Everything matters. Everything has meaning. Everyone teaches you. **REMEMBER:** Unconditional Positive Regard. *What do you see when you see people?*

4. **Allow your stories to be open to new interpretation.** When you tell a story, follow these steps. First, pause when you're finished. Give the people listening to you the space they need to process and contribute. Next, let feedback in. Listen. Consider new lessons you could have learned from the story. Play with newfound applicability. Then, write these new interpretations down. And thank people for adding value to your experience by saying, "I never would have thought of that!" or "Cool! Another lesson." *Are your stories up for discussion?*

5. **Ask for time to think about what they have said.** This is another great move for making space in the conversation. It also prevents foot in mouth disease by buying you some time to process. That way you can react less and respond more. What's more, it builds a sense of curiosity and excitement in the mind of the listener, making you more listenable. **REMEMBER:** Don't be so quick to rush into the silence. *How do you answer questions?*

6. **Be a rock people can count on.** That means stillness. That means emotional objectivity. That means listening with the ears of your heart. That means not interrupting, fixing, judging or taking over the conversations. That means staying solid to your core and reflecting people's realities back to them so they can process their own solutions. *Whom are you a rock to?*

7. **Develop the capacity for self-observation.** Become the audience of your own drama, not just the actor. That way you can better understand how people experience you, as well as how they experience themselves when they're with you. *What side of the stage are you on?*

8. **Disagreeing is tolerable – disagreeing without proposing solutions isn't.** Think of it as a Positivity Ratio: Every time you disagree, promise yourself and your team that you'll always bring two or three solutions along with you. That keeps receptivity high. *Are your disagreements derailments or springboards?*

9. **Don't be threatened by people who are smarter than you.** Otherwise you'll end up keeping people around you that are inadequate so you feel better about yourself. And that only leads to poor performance. *Are you willing to be the dummest guy in the room?*

10. **Don't develop an unwillingness to be wrong.** It doesn't look good on you. It also annoys the crap out of people. Instead, dare to be dumb. Risk being proved wrong. It makes you more approachable, more askable, more listenable and more relatable. *When was the last time you said, "I was wrong" in front of a group?*

11. **Don't communicate in a way that people have to decipher your hieroglyphics.** Write and speak with Meaningful Concrete Immediacy. Make it relevant, make it concise, and make it NOW. People will listen IF you speak in a way that doesn't require them to hire an interpreter. *Are you talking like an Egyptian?*

12. **Eventually, get people to follow you just to see where you're going.** That's trust. That's loyalty. That's inspiration. And none of it can happen without your proven track record of credibility, the engine of which is consistent, massive action. *What action have you taken today?*

13. **Find a place to shape your thoughts.** Maybe by journaling. Maybe via the laboratory that is your conversations. Maybe through ranting into a digital recorder and having your words transcribed. Doesn't matter. Form isn't as important as function. What matters is that you customize a process for constantly clarifying your thinking before publicly articulating it. Otherwise you'll sound about as eloquent as George W. Bush. *What ideas have you rounded out today?*

14. **Flap some sense into people.** By being an occasional interrogator. By being an elbow-in-the-ribs devil's advocate. Or by being a candid deliverer of painful truth. Whatever it takes. Hey, some people could use a collar-grabbing wake up call. *For whom are you an alarm clock?*

15. **Leave room for you (and others) to be human and imperfect.** Then, from that space, you connect with the intimate energy of mutual vulnerability. That's when people can stop bullshitting each other and start getting honest with each other. And that's when the lights begin to turn on. *Are you an imperfectionist?*

16. **Plan a campaign against your weakness.** That doesn't mean weakness is an awful thing. Or something you should be ashamed of. Or something you should spend all of your time and energy trying to eradicate. Instead, planning a campaign against your weakness could be as simple is acknowledging it and then delegating it. Or focusing on strengthening your strengths. Or setting a goal to ask for help more often. *Where do you suck?*

17. **Retain ongoing openness to your misguided perceptions.** First, find out how people feel around you. How they feel walking away from you. How they feel about themselves in relation to you. And how they feel when you walk into the room. You might have to run a formal evaluation to do so. Next, compare those results with your own blind spots. Identify the gaps

between who you (think) you are and what people get when they get you. Then dedicate yourself to narrowing that gap. *What barriers have you unconsciously erected?*

18. **Soften your position.** Stop being right and start being flexible. Stop being argumentative and start being accepting. Stop being defensive and start being deeply democratic. Finally, stop being unimpeachable and start being imperfect. It makes interacting with you SO much more enjoyable. **REMEMBER:** Soft is strong. *What's your default position?*

LET ME ASK YA THIS: How could you begin living your legacy of openness today?

mold your brain.

In my career, I've been blessed with a number of invaluable mentors, many of whom you've met in this book. Jeffrey Gitomer, fellow author and speaker, is man whose words have served as piercing bells of awareness in my business. Every time we hang out, he never fails to look me straight in the eye, say something staggering like "writing is the basis of all wealth," and then pause for ten seconds while the words profoundly penetrate my soul. Wow.

Here are six ways you can start LIVING this attribute today:

1. **Pause and wait.** After offering suggestions, questions, advice or ideas to people, shut up. Allow your words to profoundly penetrate them. Don't step on the silence and dilute the message. Just wait. They'll get it.

2. **Write and wait.** "Randy, I'm going to write down three words on your notebook, and I want you to just think about them." This little exercise works because it allows the words to speak on their own. Plus, the act of writing is a way to permanently etch a particular philosophy onto someone's brain. Powerful stuff.

3. **Don't recommend; GIVE.** Think about the ten books that changed your life. Then, instead of telling someone, "I've got a great book recommendation for you," go out and actually buy a copy of one of those books for them. On the inside cover, write them a personal note of inspiration. Then hand it to them in person.

4. **Practice your questioning from a better place.** Ideally, from a place of seeking to understand. *To learn. To listen. To grow. To help.* Unfortunately, too many leaders, managers and consultants will ask questions from a place of subtle, suppressed insight or camouflaged advice. As Dilbert creator Scott Adams says, "Read my mind and then recommend the decision I've already decided on."

5. **Electrify people's thinking.** Take longer pauses in your conversation. Pausing creates space, space enables clarity, and clarity eases the mind. Examples: Remember to pause before you give an answer, after you ask a question, when someone else is on a roll or after powerful insights. Then, allow YOUR words to profoundly penetrate others.

6. **Capture people's imagination.** Don't give advice; tell stories. Don't puke your boring company history; travel back in time with customers. Don't give lectures; paint pictures. Einstein was right: Imagination is more important than knowledge. *Are you boring people? Bueller? Bueller? Bueller?*

Have you ever audited your consistency?

Consistency – despite convenience and comfort – creates uncracked character.

Unfortunately, I can't teach you (or your company) how to be or stay consistent. What I *can* do is give you some questions to ask yourself, your coworkers and your organization that will increase the PROBABILITY of consistency.

Consistency between:
Your actions and your attitude.
Your behavior and your beliefs.
Your bold moves and your brand.

That's what encourages people to LISTEN TO you.

Consistency between:
Your choices and your core.
Your decisions and your dominant reality.
Your message and your mentality.

That's what enables people to TRUST IN you.

Consistency between:
Your practices and your principles.
Your projects and your philosophies.
Your vocation and your values.

That's what inspires people to FOLLOW AFTER you.

Consistency between:
Your ventures and your visions.
Your situations and your strengths.
Your terminology and your truth.

That's what impels people to TALK ABOUT you

Think you would benefit from that? Think your organization would benefit from that?

Cool.

It's time to run your Consistency Audit. The questions below are broken down into seven categories: Purpose, Values, Vision, Identity, Brand, Life and Perception.

Feel free to approach them from an organizational OR an individual level. Adjust the pronouns accordingly!

1. Consistency of PURPOSE.
Because usefulness is worship. And leaders who are called – not driven – are the ones who make the most change in the world. So, don't start a business – start a movement. Don't make money – make history. And don't do your job – validate your existence.

ASK YOURSELF:
- Am I acting from character and purpose, or is this behavior a coping mechanism to a situation?
- Am I willing to have all decisions judged in accordance with this purpose?
- How does this relate to my life purpose?
- What continually deflects me from my certainty of purpose?
- What is essential to my sense of being on purpose?
- What percentage of my time do I feel that I'm in alignment with my calling?
- What three things am I doing regularly that don't serve or support my vision, calling or purpose?
- What would REAL fulfillment look like in this area if I were truly living my life purpose?

2. Consistency of VALUES.
Because people buy people first. And customers don't buy from, trust in, or remain loyal to, companies or organizations; but to people. Also, on an internal level, people don't quit jobs – they quit people.

ASK YOURSELF:

- Am I on a path that aligns my actions to my values?
- Is this consistent with my values?
- What non-negotiables need to be honored here?
- What could I do differently to better align my responses with my values?
- What values really matter to me enough that I'm willing to sacrifice for them?
- What would I protest publicly?
- Will this action move me closer to honoring my values or further away?
- What obstacles or threats might prevent me from staying consistent to the core vision?

3. Consistency of VISION.

Because imagination is everything. Because the HOW isn't as important as the WHAT or the WHY. Because, at the risk of sounding cheesy, thoughts really DO become things. Especially when you write those thoughts down.

ASK YOURSELF:

- If everybody did exactly what I said, what would the world look like?
- Is my current action anchored in my vision?
- Is what I'm doing right now consistent with my #1 goal?
- Is what I'm telling people to do right now providing them with the tools they need to build that world I envision?
- On a scale of 1-10, how well does what I'm about to do connect to the overarching vision?
- What can I do to make this agree with my vision?
- What is the most important thing I can do to bring my activities in line with my values and vision?
- What would be most consistent with your vision in this situation?

4. Consistency of IDENTITY,

Because the goal is to bring more of yourself to every experience. To goal is to stay aligned with the working model of your identity. And the goal is to ask yourself, "What would I do in this situation? Ultimately, the goal is to think about what it would look like to "pull a YOU."

ASK YOURSELF:

- Am I behaving in a manner that is consistent with my self-concept?
- Am I being the ME I always wanted to become?
- How would the person I'm trying to become do what I'm about to do?
- How is this helping me become more of my own adjective?
- If I were ME, what would I do in this situation?
- What does this situation need of me that only I can contribute?
- What would be SO typical of me in this situation?

- What would the earlier version of me do in this situation?
- What behaviors are preventing me from making progress towards becoming the best and highest version of myself?

5. Consistency of BRAND.

Brands are shortcuts. Expectations. Predictable moments of YOU-ness. And the secret isn't to sell or market or advertise, but rather to transfer the emotion and passion and love of that which is non-average and non-boring.

ASK YOURSELF:

- Are the very first words out of my mouth consistent with my brand?
- How might this become an off-brand choice?
- How will I stamp this with my brand?
- If I decided to do this, would it support my empire?
- Is what I'm doing right now consistent with building my brand?
- What is the extension of my being, and am I exerting it here?
- Will this choice successfully express the personality of my brand?
- What could I say, do or BE – in this situation – that would simultaneously keep me in alignment with my truth, yet position me as the complete opposite of everyone else?
- Will this choice add the necessary blocks to build the brand that I want?

6. Consistency of LIVING.

Because people are listening to your life speak. People are watching what you DO. And the goal is to make your life the work of art, using YOU as the medium. Paint is for amateurs anyway.

ASK YOURSELF:

- Am I currently speaking from a place of personal truth?
- Are my actions predictable and congruent with my stated positions?
- How have I already done and become what I'm about to teach?
- How well is this statement reflected in my life right now?
- Is how I'm behaving right now consistent with the attitude I strive to maintain?
- Is the message I'm currently preaching the dominant reality of my life?
- Is the statement I'm making with my life consistent with my heart?
- What (specifically) do I need to have already done or become in order to confidently preach this message without people questioning my credibility?

7. Consistency of PERCEPTION.

Because what people remember about you is what you are. And that depends on how people experience you. It also depends on how people experience themselves when they're with you. And it depends on what people think when they see your name.

ASK YOURSELF:
- How deep is the gap between my onstage performance and my backstage reality?
- If I did this, would the result in any way enhance my perception as a jack-of-all-trades?
- If I partook in this experience – and people saw me – would they perceive me as being out of alignment with my true self?
- If I proceeded with this endeavor, would people who know me have ANY question in their mind that it came from me?
- If my best clients and closest friends saw me doing this, would it be seen as a compromise of integrity?
- Once we're finished with the project, would this client be a good commercial for my business?
- Would I want to become known for what I'm about to do?

FINAL CHALLENGE: If you completed the audit and noticed more areas of inconsistency then you'd like to have, that's a good thing.

You don't have to live your life as a walking contradiction if you don't want to.

Instead, to bring your inner and outer worlds into harmony, consider these final questions:

How far can I deviate before crossing the line that puts me into inconsistent territory?
What kind of structure can I place around myself to make sure I remember to do this consistently?
What support would I need to have in place in order to remember that I have a choice?

REMEMBER: Nobody can "force" consistency upon you or your organization.

THE GOOD NEWS IS: By running this audit; you great increase the PROBABILITY of being and staying consistent.

Because if there's one thing I've learned from wearing a nametag for the past ten years, it's that consistency is far better than rare moments of greatness.

HELLO
MY NAME IS CHAPTER,

forty-five

If you were the most consistent person you knew, how would your organization be different?

Now that you've audited your consistency, here's a rapid-fire list of practices for staying consistent:

1. **ACT** in harmony with the way you see yourself. That's the big assignment. And it's not an easy one to take on.

2. **ALIGN** your responses with your values. That way you won't have to try to remember what you said.

3. **ASK** what would be so typical of you to do in this situation. Then do that. Establish enough predictability that you can prove people's expectations every time.

4. **ASSURE** the first words out of your mouth are consistent with your brand. So much so that when you answer the phone, people nod and smile at your seamlessness.

5. **BE** The You you've always wanted to become. After all, living falsehoods is exhausting. And with the exception of Danny Ganz, Dana Carvey and Frank Caliendo, impressionists rarely make it big.

6. **BEHAVE** (right now) consistent with the attitude you strive to maintain. Otherwise people will not listen to your words because they'll be too busy examining the character deficiency within your actions.

7. **CHOOSE** what few things you will consistently make part of your life, regardless of the circumstances. These become your non-negotiables. Your must-haves, must-do's and must-be's.

8. **DECIDE** if this choice will bring you closer to the highest version of yourself. If it won't, consider making a different one. Life's too short.

9. **DETERMINE** what values & aspirations you want your behaviors to be aligned with. Then keep them typed out on a little laminated card in you wallet.

10. **DO** what a cool company would do in this situation. Because cool companies get noticed, get remembered and GET business. And that's good for business.

11. **DO** what consistency would do in this situation. Because consistency is far better than rare moments of greatness. Not to mention, it's a hell of a lot easier.

12. **DO** what the person you are trying to become would do. This brings you one step closer. One chisel smack away from revealing the sculpture inside the stone.

13. **DO** what YOU would do in this situation. Wear a bracelet that reads, "WWID?" That should start some interesting conversations.

14. **DO** whatever you have to do to make this agree with your vision. And after a while, if you still can't match the two up, bag it.

15. **ENGAGE** only in activities that support your empire. Everything else is a waste of time, money, energy and brainpower.

16. **GIVE** to this situation that which you alone can offer. Preferably, that which you were designed to cure. That which you are known for knowing. That which you can't help but doing and being.

17. **GO** out of your way to ME-ize this moment. Stamp it with the emblem of YOU.

18. **IMAGINE** what it would mean and look like to be true to your values here. That will most likely impel you into action.

19. **KEEP** on the path that aligns your actions to your values. It has the best view, the fewest potholes and the least amount of litter.

20. **LET** the best YOU come across in this situation. Any other version is robbing other people of experiencing your awesomeness.

21. **LISTEN** to who you are before responding. That split second pause might actually improve your answer.

22. **MAKE** choices that add wood to your internal fire. Then watch that baby burn, burn burn.

23. **MOVE** in a way that honors your soul. Because that will actually honor OTHER people's souls too.

24. **PLACE** structure around yourself to make sure you remember what to do consistently. Sticky notes work. Mantras written on the wall work. Silicone bracelets work.

25. **PONDER** what the earlier version of yourself would have done in this situation. Then decide if the current version of yourself knows a better way.

26. **PRACTICE** bringing a little more of yourself to every situation. Not too much. Just enough that you walk away thinking, "I really felt like MYSELF back there."

27. **PREACH** the message that is the dominant reality of your life. Otherwise people will not listen to you because of the non-stop noise of your character deficiency.

28. **REMEMBER** that flawless execution doesn't exist. Make mistakes, make them early and make them quick. Write them down and what you learned. Then keep moving.

29. **SPEAK** from a place of personal truth. It makes you more listenable.

30. **STAMP** everything with you do with your brand, or else don't bother doing it. After all, what happens when everybody loves it, but doesn't know who made it?

31. **STAY** in alignment with the best working model of your identity. Which means you should probably create that model first.

32. **STRIVE** to behave in a manner that is consistent with your self-concept. It's hard to do but it will serve you well.

33. **USE** this experience to continuing becoming the highest version of yourself. Because that's the only version people will benefit from.

REMEMBER: Consistency is far better than rare moments of greatness.

HELLO
MY NAME IS CHAPTER,

forty-six

How do you
make decisions?

Ever seen people sport those bracelets that read, "W.W.J.D?"

They stand for "What would Jesus do?"

I remember when they got big in the 90's. In fact, they're still popular today.

Interestingly, I recently found out that this well-known phrase, deriving from the Latin *imitatio dei*, or "the imitation of God," didn't gain cultural popularity until 1896.

Credit goes to Charles Sheldon's book, *In His Steps*, in which the subtitle was, "What Would Jesus Do?"

Anyway, that got me thinking. Not about Jesus or Christianity or religion.

But about making decisions. And HOW and WHY we make those decisions.

What about you? Have you ever thought about how and why YOU make decisions?

Because:

If you TRULY want to convey a thorough understanding of yourself…
If you HONESTY want to create a good working model of your own identity…
If you SINCERELY want to maintain consistency and alignment of your actions…

You need to consider *how you decide.*

From the minute choices you make throughout the day, to your annual goal setting activities, to your major entreprenerial or career decisions.

All of these choices fall under the umbrella of your Personal Guidance System. Your Opportunity Filter. Your Decision Tree of Life.

Now, you might not CALL it any of those things. In fact, I'd be willing to bet that less than 10% of the population has ever sat down and physically mapped out how they decide.

And for that reason, my challenge for you today is:

Physically create a governing document for your daily decision-making.

I just stumbled upon this process about six months ago myself. And I assure you it's one of – if not THEE – most powerful exercises I've EVER executed for creating a good working model of my own identity.

Here's how to do it:

1. **Retrace your steps.** Start by making a list of *every single choice* you made yesterday. What you ate, how you listened to people, which tasks your invested your time in, EVERYTHING. From the moment you woke up to the moment you went to bed. Now, obviously, you won't be able to record EVERY choice. Just do the best you can.

2. **Evaluate your process.** For each item on your list, go back and think about HOW you actually made that choice. Ask yourself questions like:

   a) Why did I make that choice?
   b) What alternatives did I decide against?
   c) Whom or what did I model my choice after?
   d) What questions did I ask myself before choosing?
   e) What thought processes did I take myself through?

   It's just like being a contestant on *Millionaire:* Four answers. Three lifelines. And you explain your decision-making process in real time to the host and audience so you can make an informed decision. "Well Regis, I know the answer's not Lithuania because I've visited that country before … and I don't think the answer is Latvia because I did paper on their government when I was in college, so…"

3. **Dig for values.** Once you've uncovered the HOW for each of yesterday's decisions, it's time to find out WHY. Ask yourself questions like:

   a) What values were those choices rooted in?
   b) What commonalities did all of my choices contain?
   c) Where did I learn how to make that kind of choice?
   d) And what words governed the questions I asked myself when I made those choices?

4. **Categorize and document.** OK! At this point, you should have a pretty solid idea HOW and WHY you make decisions. The final step is to map out your Official Governing Document. You can name it whatever you like, i.e., "Sara's Personal Guidance System,""Mark's Opportunity Filter,""Deb's Decision Tree," whatever.

   Now, in terms of design, that's entirely up to you. Depending on your learning/personality style, you might try mind-maps, decision trees, self-talk scripts, affirmations or visual thinking diagrams. Personally, the structure I used was twofold:

   FIRST: Extract the ten core philosophies/values/virtues behind all of my choices, i.e.,"Writing is the basis of all wealth."
   SECOND: List all the questions I might ask myself that reflect such values, i.e., "Is everything you know written down somewhere?"

5. **Reinforcement and accountability.** Cool. You've assembled your governing document for daily decisions making. Now, keep in mind – this WILL change over time, as your values will change over time. So, be sure to think of it as a draft. Meanwhile, if you really want to blow people away, I challenge you to keep a copy of this document in your wallet or on your office wall. Look at it daily. Share it with those who inquire. Do this exercise with a partner or team if you want. Not only will these measures keep you accountable and consistent, but they will also inspire all who see it to make a similar self-assessment of their own decision-making.

REMEMBER: The ONLY thing in this world you have ANY control over … *is your choice.*

So, doesn't it make sense to map out HOW and WHY you make those choices?

Doesn't it make sense to start asking yourself,"W.W.I.D?" or"What would I do?"

I wonder if we can find any bracelets that say THAT.

HELLO
MY NAME IS CHAPTER,

forty-seven

What if you practiced everything?

Halfway through the movie *The Peaceful Warrior*, Nick Nolte's character, Socrates, makes a profound point about practicing:

"That's the difference between me and you, Danny," he explains to his young apprentice, "You practice gymnastics. I practice EVERYTHING."

SO, MY QUESTION FOR YOU IS: What are YOU practicing?

Now, I bet if you asked a hundred people, their answers might include activities like: musical scales, free-throws or magic tricks; listening, patience or question-asking; and mediation, mindfulness or yoga.

And I would say, "Good." Because all of those things are important to practice.

BUT MY CHALLENGE TO YOU IS: Rethink your definition of the word "practice."

Because it's not just a word. It's not just some action you do repeatedly for twenty minutes a day.

It's a religion. And by that I don't mean "The Divine" or "Your Personal Faith," but rather *whatever your life is dedicated most to.*

So, the follow-up question to, "What are you practicing?" is:

How could you approach everything you do as practice?

Wow. What a concept.

This goes WAY beyond practicing musical scales or magic tricks.

We're talking about practicing LIFE.
We're talking about practicing BEING YOURSELF.
We're talking about practicing YOUR CHERISHED VALUES.

Yes, all of these things can be practiced.

But only if your definition of the word, "practice" evolves.

If you're focused on the process, not the product.
If you're focused on the journey, not the destination.
If you're focused deepening and enhancing, not achieving and bettering.

Because you're not striving for perfection.

You're not striving at all.

You're just DOING. Just BEING.

You're not waiting for The Main Event, The Big Competition or Game Day.

EVERY day is game day. Every moment is game moment. And NOW, this present experience, IS practice. For its own sake. For the love of practice.

*   *   *   *   *

My education in the religion of practice has evolved from three key periods in my life:

ONE: MUSIC
I first understood the value of practice when I began playing, composing, recording and performing music at the age of 12. My dad, who taught me music – both the art of appreciating AND playing it – said it best: "You just have to play everyday."

That's it. You don't need lessons. You don't need Mel Bay Book 2. Just play every day. Whether it's for five minutes or five hours.
Practicing music is just what musicians DO.

As BB King once said, "If I forget to practice one day, only I will be able to tell. But if I forget practice two days in a row, my audience will be able to tell."

TWO: WRITING

I further understood the value of practice when I started my company in 2002. As a writer, all my mentors' advice all pointed to the same thing: "A writer writes. Always."

So, you practice writing. Every single day, without exception. It doesn't matter if you create one line, one page or one chapter on that day.

Practicing writing is just what writers DO.

As my favorite author, Steven Pressfield once said, "All that matters is having the courage to sit down a try, every day."

THREE: YOGA

Then, in 2008, my philosophy evolved to a new level. Once I started practicing yoga, THAT act became the vehicle for awakening to the TRUE value of practice.

Yoga rocked my world. It shook my soul. It changed me forever. Physically, mentally, spiritually and emotionally. And the cool part was, as a student of yoga, I learned that you don't "go to yoga class."

You go to practice.

It's a noun AND a verb.

Pretty cool, huh?

AND HERE'S THE BEST PART: You never "get better" at anything.

You only ENHANCE your practice.
You only DEEPEN your practice.

Every day. Even if you can't make it into the studio every day. After all, your yoga "practice" is isn't something that's limited to the studio.

Practicing is just what yogis DO.

As hatha yoga guru Bikram Choudhry says, "It's never too late, it's never too bad, and you're never too old or too sick to start from scratch once again."

*   *   *   *   *

So, as my philosophy of practice has evolved, I've started to ask myself a few NEW questions. For example:

Wouldn't it be cool if you could practice LIFE?
Wouldn't it be cool if you could practice LIVING?
Wouldn't it be cool if you could practice BEING?

Not to achieve anything. Not to prepare for anything. *Just for the practice.*

Wouldn't it be cool to shift your attitude in a way that, at ANY POINT during the day, if someone called your cell phone and asked, "So, what are you up to right now?" you could ALWAYS respond with, "Just practicing"?

Because, simply out of curiosity, your friend on the other end of the phone would HAVE to ask, "Oh yeah? What are you practicing?"

"Life."

Whoa.

You'd blow people's minds.

Simply because you made the conscious decision to practice EVERYTHING.

Because the world is your studio.

So, allow me to repeat those same two questions from earlier:

What are you practicing?
How could you approach everything you do as practice?

With those ideas in mind, let's explore a list of uncommon practices.

Some are attitudes. Some are activities. Some are states of being.

All are practices; none are common.

SO, CAUTION: Please don't kill yourself trying to incorporate each one of these into your daily life.

Instead, I challenge you to embrace the individual practices that catch your eye. The ones that alter the speed of your pulse. The ones that connect with who you are at your core:

1. **Practice accepting compliments.** How you respond to a compliment speaks volumes about your self-esteem, personality and state of being. Some people justify. Some people deflect. Some people giggle. Some people simply say, "Thank you." *Which one are you?*

2. **Practice aggressive pondering.** My best friend, Andy Masters, taught me this one. You might say he's a "master" of this practice. Aggressive pondering can be designed around YOUR thinking and learning style. Whether you make lists, journal, sit on a beach, meditate in a cave, draw on flip charts or scatter hundreds of colored note cards across the carpet (my fave!), the challenge is to think. To really, really think. About whatever you want. *How much time each day do you spend just thinking?*

3. **Practice being happy.** Throughout your day, seek out specific things to observe that you KNOW will make you smile. Personally, I use kids and pets. Perfect vehicles for spontaneous happiness. It's almost impossible NOT to smile when you see them, which means it's impossible NOT to be happy. Also, if you're fortunate enough to spend your waking hours engaged in something that you're passionate about; I challenge you to step back every hour or so to simply drink in the moment and say to yourself, "This moment is perfect. I am perfect. I am happiness." *What made you smile this morning?*

4. **Practice being yourself.** Of course, the secret to this practice is first KNOWING yourself. That's a big enough challenge as it is. So, here's what you do. Think of three specific things, thoughts, behaviors or attitudes that you believe to be unique to YOU. Maybe it's the questions you ask, maybe it's the boundaries you set, or maybe it's the values by which you live. Whatever you choose, solidify those attributes as the foundation of your BEING. Then, in to practice being yourself, constantly ask the great question made famous by author/speaker/thinker Jim Cathcart: *How would the person I'm trying to become do what I'm about to do?*

5. **Practice confident uncertainty.** In Ellen Langer's classic book, *Mindfulness,* she defined this practice gorgeously. So, let me just quote a few of her key points on the idea: Confident uncertainty … legitimizes curiosity. Confident uncertainty … enables people construct the experience. Confident uncertainty … is conducive to innovation and initiative. Confident uncertainty … breeds independent judgment and a general freedom of action. Confident uncertainty … leads to a search for more information, and with more

information there may be more options. *How many of the decisions you make each day have absolutely correct answers?*

6. **Practice constructive solitude.** Take a walk. Take a run. Take a swim. Sit in the corner of Starbucks with a book. Take a week off work and go to Sedona and don't talk to ANYBODY (my fave!) Solitude is precious. It cures stress. It sorts ideas. It is a restoration that resonates resolution. And the best part is, creativity adores it. *Are you giving yourself permission to be alone?*

7. **Practice inner attention.** Every answer to every problem that ever arises in your life can be found by paying exquisite attention to yourself. To your body. To your mind. To your emotions. To your intuition. There are endless paths for doing so, from yoga to chanting mantras to praying to TM to journaling. *How well are you listening to yourself?*

8. **Practice intense relaxation.** Believe it or not, we have to teach ourselves how to relax. I know, it sounds dumb. But take it from someone who was hospitalized three times in six months because he didn't know how to relax. Yep. Simultaneously the stupidest mistake AND the most glorious awakening of my life. And the best part is: now I've finally learned how to relax. Whether it's meditating, mini-vacations, taking walks or watching *Dumb & Dumber* for the 179th time, it works for me. And that's the key. You need to discover what works for you without overly regimenting anything. *How did you relax yesterday?*

9. **Practice intentional discomfort.** Comfort zones are overrated. You have absolutely NO business there. If you want to learn, you've GOT to stick yourself out there. All day. Every day. Literally. Metaphorically. Spiritually. Emotionally. In person. Online. On paper. On stage. *What did you do yesterday that scared you?*

10. **Practice intentional silence.** Whether it's on paper, on stage or in conversation … pausing … is one of the great forces in the universe. Pausing applies pressure. Pausing creates space. Pausing evokes emotions. Pausing invites learning. Pausing examines nuances. Pausing communicates empathy. Pausing attracts attention. Pausing demonstrates respect. Pausing facilitates idea penetration. *Are leaving enough space between words?*

11. **Practice irrepressible resilience.** Determination. Commitment. Discipline. Perseverance. Stick-to-itiveness. Bouncing Back. Getting up. Not backing down. Refusing to go away. All that stuff. Same thing. Same practice. You can do this one all day, in every endeavor. *How are you building your resiliency?*

12. Practice joyful service. There is no other way to serve. There is no other way to live. What's more, when you bring joy into the service process, customers LOVE it. They have to – it's contagious. It oozes out of you and coats the concrete on which you and your customers stand. *How much loyalty are you sacrificing by NOT incorporating joy into your service process?*

13. Practice mattering daily. It's healthy. It builds character. It reinforces your self-esteem. If you can find a way to validate your existence on a daily basis, you'll never waste another day in your life. And, by the way, I can guarantee that you DO matter. To someone or some THING, you matter. *Are you, on a daily basis, doing stuff that matters?*

14. Practice mental evacuations. Thinking is the great paradox: It's the greatest thing man has achieved, yet it's the single thing that's going to destroy our civilization. Because of that, I challenge you to evacuate, to DUMP your mind on a regular basis. Now, that doesn't mean DISPLACE your mind by getting stoned or drunk every other night. I said DUMP. Which means take out the trash. As aforementioned *Peaceful Warrior* suggests, "The trash is anything that takes you away from the present moment." *What mental obstacles are preventing you from being an effective person?*

15. Practice non-manipulative intentionality. People can smell manipulation from a mile a way. And if you telegraph your neediness, they won't (1) Listen TO you, (2) Buy FROM you, or (3) Trust IN you. So, just relax. Persuade manipulation-free and earn trust trick-free. *Are you harmonizing or manipulating?*

16. Practice not doing. Maybe a little more BEING. After all, people aren't going to be influenced by what you believe or say (or even) DO. They'll be influenced by WHO YOU ARE. Less doing, more being. *What does who-you-are tell people?*

17. Practice participatory management. Stop dominating. Stop dictating. Stop doing and saying things AT people. Try WITH them instead. They might actually listen to you. *How are you creating an environment where healthy participation naturally emerges?*

18. Practice positive DOING. Nothing against Normal Vincent Peale. But, seriously. Positive thinking doesn't make you money. It might give you an unstoppable attitude, but only ACTION … only EXECUTION is priceless. *What actions can you take TODAY to eliminate or minimize barriers to your boldness?*

19. Practice positive negativity. Speaking of positive attitudes, also remember that being a little negative can go a LONG way. Especially if it's rooted in a healthy dose of doubt. Doubt protects us. Doubt gives us choices. Doubt is smart. *Are you beginning with it?*

20. Practice posture maintenance. First, literally. Beware of your shoulders sneaking their way up to your ears. Second, metaphorically. Beware of the way in which you walk in this world. Your posture – your attitude, your carriage, your approach – says a LOT about you. *What do people get when they get you?*

21. Practice proactive gratitude. If you're not writing in a Gratitude Journal every day, you're a putz. Perhaps that's why stuff hasn't been going you way. Because you're not giving enough thanks. Remember, that which you appreciate appreciates. *What ten things are you thankful for today?*

22. Practice random thinking. Structure is overrated. Give yourself permission to just sit and think. About whatever comes to your mind. You may even consider doing so on PAPER, just in case you come up with something that's GOLD JERRY GOLD! *How much time yesterday do you spend just thinking?*

23. Practice regular past shedding. You are not your past. That's not your identity, that's not what matters, and that's not now what people care about. Let it go. Think of yourself as a snake whose skin requires seasonal shedding. *What have you recently let go of?*

24. Practice responsible anarchy. Order is (also) overrated. Craziness, chaos and rebellion, on the other hand, are much healthier. They put hair on your chest. They build character. *How many waves did you make last week?*

25. Practice strategic serendipity. Luck doesn't exist. Luck is an acronym for "Working Your Ass Off." So, find out where the rock created the ripple and then go throw more rocks. And if you want to be in the right place at the right time, you need to be in a lot of places. *How many places are YOU in?*

26. Practice taking crap. Not only is it healthy for your ego, but it also trains you to respond instead of react. To judge whether or not this person's criticism has any merit. In the words of my mentor, Jeffrey Gitomer, "If they have a nicer car than me, then I'll listen to their criticism." *How patient are you willing to be?*

27 **Practice talking normally.** Like a person, not a robot. Like a human, not a script. Normalize, standardize and internalize your thoughts through writing, then share them with the world in a language your 11 year-old daughter could understand. *Are you speaking simply enough?*

28. **Practice the presence.** Especially when you're listening. Focus on the breath. Focus the other person's immediate experience. Focus on how their words have an effect on you. Also, when you're not listening, you can do the same. Find a way to incorporate deep breathing into everything you do. *Is your presence calming others?*

29. **Practice uncalculated generosity.** Trash the scorecard. Just starting being kind to people for no reason and with no agenda. People will notice. *Whose lunch did you buy this week?*

30. **Practice with everybody.** Especially the people who are better than you. They will teach you, they will inspire you and they will keep you accountable. Also, don't overlook the value of practicing with beginners. They will keep you humble and help you recognize how far you've come. *Who are you afraid to practice next to?*

31. **Practice with passion.** Last point. Most important point. PASSION. It makes the time go by faster. It makes it more fun. It makes it NOT feel like practice. Remember, it's not "the way you practice is the way you play." If you practice EVERYTHING, then "the way you practice is the way you ARE." *When was the last time you lost track of time while practicing?*

REMEMBER: Practice, practice, practice!

Not an act. Not a habit. Not a "thing you do every morning."

A religion. A philosophy. A way of life.

I challenge you to rethink your definition of the word "practice."

Learn to practice everything.
Learn to approach everything you do as an opportunity to practice SOMETHING.

When you walk out of a room, how does it change?

Five words that will change your business forever:

"Who was that masked man?"

Name that show!

Of course: *The Lone Ranger*. Even a Gen-Xer like me knows that.

And just imagine. Wouldn't it be cool if customers said something like that after YOU left?

Curiosity. Intrigue. Fascination. Amazement.

That's what those five words represent. The Lone Ranger was so cool, so unforgettable, and so distinctive that when he left, people wanted more.

AND SO, HERE'S THE BIG QUESTION: When you walk out of a room, how does it change?

SEE, HERE'S THE SECRET: Whatever change occurs to the room is a tangible representation of how your character, actions, words, reputation and personality have been experienced by the people around you.

The following list explores several possibilities of how a room might change when you walk out of it. As you explore these examples, ask yourself which of them best applies to you, or which ones you'd LIKE to apply to you:

1. **When you walk out of a room, are people genuinely sad to see you go?** In a 2009 Daily Show interview with Michael J. Fox, Jon Stewart wrapped the conversation up with the following compliment, "Michael, when you walk into a room, everybody feels better." Wow. Sure is inspiring to see someone have that kind of effect on people. And I imagine that if YOU did, your career would surely skyrocket.

   Unfortunately, some individuals are the opposite: *Everybody feels better when they walk OUT of a room.* And the silent dialogue becomes, "I'm so glad she finally left," "I thought she'd NEVER leave!" or, worst of all, "Thank God that guy's gone. Now we can relax." This is not good. If your leaving the room results in people's postures relaxing as they breathe a hefty sigh of relief, you're doing something wrong. If your leaving the room allows people to (finally) resume their conversations, you're doing something wrong. *Do you bring drama or peace into people's lives?*

2. **When you walk out of a room, does the population of that room decrease?** That's the epitome of leadership: People want to walk out of the room and follow you, even if they have no idea where you're going. That's also a surefire sign of presence: People just assume go home now that you've left the party. Because you're inspiring. Because you're trustworthy. Because you're fun to talk to. And because you're followable. I wonder what you would have to think, say, do or BE differently in order to make that happen. *How are you leaving an imprint on everyone you meet?*

3. **When you walk out of a room, does the temperature go up five degrees?** This reminds me of SNL's Debbie Downer, brilliantly played by Rachel Dratch. Her cynical character's sole purpose was to interrupt social gatherings to voice negative opinions and pronouncements. She immediately sucked the energy level out of the room like a Hoover vacuum. And ever time she did so; the classic "Wa-Wa" trumpet sound effect would play. *Are you like that?* Someone who persistently adds bad news or negative feelings to a gathering, thus bringing down the mood of everyone around you? I hope not. Because Debbie Downers are avoided like the plague. And when they walk out of a room, people are GLAD to see them go. Because negatively rarely looks good on anybody. *What is the temperature of your presence?*

4. **When you walk out of a room, do people ask about you?** This brings us back to The Lone Ranger. His departure stimulated curiosity, intrigue, fascination and amazement. Now, obviously you can't expect to achieve such memorable presence every time you leave a room. What you CAN do

is increase the probability of people asking about you by practicing tenets of approachability. First: Be The Observed, not The Observer. Second: Create Points of Dissonance. Third: Position yourself as a resource. And fourth: Build Name Equity. No silver bullets, horses or sidekicks necessary. *Are you buzz-worthy?*

5. **When you walk out of a room, does it get quieter?** Meet my friend Neen James. She's a productivity consultant, originally from Australia. And while it's hard to explain in writing, she has the most contagious, smile-inducing laugh you'll ever hear. She's also the type of person who can find humor in anything. So, when you're hanging out with her, you get to hear that famous laugh A LOT. Which, in turn, makes you laugh more. Which makes her laugh more. Which makes you laugh more. And the endless cycle of fun begins. Combine that with Neen's optimistic, no-worries attitude and upbeat energy, when SHE walks out of the room, the volume goes from eleven to six. Like clockwork. Which makes sense, since she IS a productivity consultant. *How fun are you pereceived as being?*

6. **When you walk out of a room, how do you leave people?** Maybe people start taking action. This means you were inspiring, interesting and actionable. Maybe people swim in mutual confusion of having no idea what the hell you just said. This means you need to speak with more Meaningful Concrete Immediacy. Or, maybe people spring to life. This means you spoke in a passionate, challenging and empowering manner. The choice is yours. *How do you leave people?*

7. **When you walk out of a room, are new people connected that otherwise wouldn't have met?** *Networkers* work the room. They deal their deck of business cards to everyone they encounter in a superficial, flaky, campaign-trail way. They're spotted from a mile away and reek of the stench of self-centered overexertion. *Connectors*, on the other hand, help the room work itself. They find people that need to meet, use accomplishment-based introductions, and then get the heck out of the way. But here's the catch: They can only be spotted from up close. Because that's the nature of their relationships: Close. That's how people are draw to them: Close. *Are you networking or connecting?*

8. **When you walk out of a room, does your spirit remain?** Lastly, this suggests you don't just want people to remember you, but to be positively influenced BY you. "Noticeable in your absence," as I like to say. And the ideal situation is, people will start to patiently and excitedly wait until they are given the privilege of being blessed with your presence again. But not

because you're always perfect. Not because you're always in performance mode. Rather, because you always make people feel essential by helping them fall in love with themselves. *How do YOU leave people?*

REMEMBER: If your presence makes a difference, your absence will make a difference too.

Ultimately, it's not about being the life of the party – it's about bringing other people TO life AT the party.

It's about leaving behind a silver-bullet trail of uncracked character that makes people wonder, "Who was that masked man?"

HELLO
MY NAME IS CHAPTER,

forty-nine

How do you leave people?

As I leave you, I'd like you to think about how YOU leave people.

Do you leave people wondering? *Because you enlisted their creativity.*

Do you leave people wanting more? *Because you emotionally engaged them.*

Do you leave people curious? *Because you built a frame of interest and intrigue.*

Do you leave people laughing? *Because you helped them evoke the humor in their own lives.*

Do you leave people inspired? *Because you enabled them to give birth to their own realizations.*

Do you leave people thinking differently about themselves? *Because you challenged them apply something to their own lives.*

Do you leave people feeling good about themselves? *Because you honored, respected and made them feel essential.*

Do you leave people thinking, in general? *Because you asked pointed, creative and penetrating questions.*

Do you leave people reevaluating? *Because something you said made them confront themselves.*

Do you leave people relieved? *Because you actually listened.*

My name is Scott.
Thanks for listening.

SCOTT GINSBERG
That Guy with the Nametag

AUTHOR. Scott's ten books including *HELLO, my name is Scott, The Power of Approachability, How to be That Guy, Make a Name for Yourself* and *Stick Yourself Out There/Get Them to Come to You,* have been featured on media outlets such as *20/20, The Wall Street Journal, USA Today, Fast Company COSMO, Redbook, The Investor's Business Daily* and *Ripley's Believe It Or Not.*

SPEAKER. Scott delivers customized presentations, breakout sessions, keynote speeches and seminars to tens of thousands of people each year. He's worked with companies like STAPLES, Verizon Wireless, Manpower, Boeing, Canada Post and The Australian Institute of Management. Every program is about always about approachability; yet every program is different. Never the same speech twice.

NAMETAGTV. Scott's Online Training Network is an interactive Learning Environment that provides public AND premium customized learning modules for entrepreneurs, salespeople, frontline employees and marketers who want to leverage approachability into profitability.

BLOGGER. In 2007, Alexa and Technorati voted *HELLO, my name is Blog!* as a "Top 100 Business Blog on the Web." With 1,200+ blog posts, every day, Scott's posts are shared and linked around the web, drawing millions of readers worldwide.

COLUMNIST. Since 2004, Scott has written over 1,000 articles and been a regular contributor to print publications like *The St. Louis Small Business Monthly, INSTORE Magazine;* Employment Info, The Ladders and dozens of online publications like RainToday and ExpertVillage.

THOUGHT LEADER. Dubbed "The Authority on Approachability," Scott is regularly featured in and interviewed by media outlets worldwide. He's been quoted on and interviewed by MSNBC, CNN, The Washington Post, The Associated Press, The Today Show and Paul Harvey. He also wrote "The Quiz" on approachability for COSMO and, in 2008, *The St. Louis Small Business Monthly* voted Scott as one of the "Top Young Entrepreneurs of the Year."

What do people hear when they listen to your life speak?